Thick Luck

THE SEARCH FOR POWS & MIAS

The characters and events in this book are not fictitious. Any similarity to real persons, living or dead, *other than specified* is coincidental and not intended by the author. Care was taken to protect the identity of any official personalities requiring such protection. Any specific reference to a POW/MIA missing or recovered service member is with the approval and consent of the family.

All photographs are personal photos other than specified.

POW/MIA loss narratives are courtesy of Mary and Chuck Schantag
P.O.W. Network
www.pownetwork.org

Bouna Books
2006

David A. Combs
www.RangerCombs.com

Thick Luck

THE SEARCH FOR POWS & MIAS

DAVID A. COMBS

Dedication

To my wife, Nyra, my best friend and the love of my life, for her unwavering support during my career as an Army Ranger and in everything I do.

To my parents Florian and Theresa Combs for their inspiration, encouragement, and support of me and my goals.

To my daughter Leilani who grew up without me because I was almost never home - my duties always kept me on the move.

HALO, my bullmastiff - my second born.

Acknowledgements

There are many people who deserve to be acknowledged for their impact on Thick Luck – The Search for POWs & MIAs.

I will always start with my parents Florian (Bud) and Theresa (Sidla) Combs. They were the absolute model of dedicated parents and set an example for discipline and moral ethics that were of the highest standard

I would also like to express my gratitude to Mr. William (Bill) Forsythe and Master Sergeant Suriyan Collins. They were my facilitators to success in finding results in the POW and MIA issues in Laos and Cambodia.

To the Soldiers, Sailors, Airmen, Marines and Civilian and Government employees of Joint Task–Force Full Accounting and the Central Identification Laboratory–Hawaii, now the Joint POW/MIA Accounting Command. Their dedication to the recovery of our missing and fallen comrades deserves the admiration and gratitude of every American. I was honored to have the privilege to serve with them.

Foreword

"I'd like to take him back and bury him in his own country . . .
"I think the dead have no nationality."
"No. But their kin do."

Cormac McCarthy's *The Crossing*

I wrote this book at the request of my mother who read my letters from around the world for many years but did not fully understand my duties and responsibilities. *"Thick Luck"* is a compilation of events and experiences during my participation in the U.S. effort to account for missing Prisoners of War and Missing in Action from the war in Southeast Asia.

Sometimes I wondered how I became involved in the hunt for America's POWs and MIAs. For three years I had the privilege to lead a team of investigation experts to Laos and Cambodia. Up to five times each year, my team would trek into the jungles to long forgotten battlefields near the Vietnam border. We searched for undiscovered burial or aircraft crash sites from the secret wars that had been waged there. Paramount was the search for any clue of an American POW or MIA still alive in Southeast Asia.

Our team was extremely successful and provided bittersweet closure and progress for the families who depended upon our work. We carried their hopes in our hearts and it cemented the resolve of our team to succeed. There was no monetary price or personal sacrifice that would keep us from completing our mission.

We understood the timeless warrior's code of depending upon each other—knowing our comrades were waiting for us to bring them home. Those missing warriors paid the ultimate sacrifice. The soldiers, sailors, airmen, and marines, of Joint Task Force-Full Accounting were now sacrificing personal safety, aspirations, family, and sometimes their lives to account for our missing. The remainder of America should be thankful for their service.

Memorial to My Father

Florian Vance Combs
Serial Number: 730-62-28
D.O.W. – Duration of the War
United States Navy
March 19, 1945

LCS 113 in Saipan, 1945.

I was a senior in high school and subject to draft upon graduation. I always wanted to join the Navy and joined in March of my senior year. The folks were pretty upset, being an only child, but they were pretty proud and attended the graduation ceremony to receive my diploma … the teachers accelerated all my classes so my grades were earned before I left.

I attended boot camp at Camp Hall, Great Lakes, Illinois and was assigned to LCS113. I was on ship APA38 from San Diego to Samar, Philippines where we were put ashore. Seven of us were flown to Fleet Headquarters on Guam and then via destroyer to Okinawa. It was during this trip that we were in the typhoon that the book "Caine Mutiny" was written about.

The atom bomb was dropped while we were at sea. We were flown to Saipan and the Tinian Islands where we caught a plane flying to Yokahoma in time for the surrender ceremony where the Japanese surrendered to MacArthur on the battleship Missouri (General Douglas MacArthur).

We spent months sweeping and destroying mines in the Korean Straits operating out of Sasebo, Japan. We brought the LCS (Landing Craft Support ship) to Pearl Harbor into dry dock and then on to Astoria, Oregon where it was decommissioned.

On Samar, Saipan and Okinawa we ran into Japanese soldiers who didn't know the war was over and were still resisting. On Samar they wounded one of our guys and on Saipan and Okinawa they were subdued before any damage was done.

It was six months from the time I shipped out from San Diego to the time I got my first mail. All the packages that had been sent were either lost or stolen. I can remember arranging the mail chronologically before I opened it.

I was discharged at the U.S. Navy Station in Minneapolis, Minnesota.

Table of Contents

Chapter 1 The Dark Side 1

Chapter 2 Land of a Million Elephants 19

Chapter 3 Into the Mist 49

Chapter 4 Into the Darkness 87

Chapter 5 Big Challenges 129

Chapter 6 The Bone Hunters 147

Chapter 7 Isolated Burials 179

Chapter 8 The Killing Fields 189

Chapter 9 Last Known Alive 207

Chapter 10 The Sacred Mountain 217

Chapter 11 Day of Reckoning 255

Epilogue 271

Glossary 273

About the Author 277

Chapter 1
The Dark Side

Fifteen years earlier I had made the decision to enlist in the U.S. Army for a four year adventure tour. I had just graduated from college with a Bachelor of Science degree but was not prepared to commit to a career in business. Therefore, I made an appointment for the next day with the local Army Recruiter in Decorah, Iowa. I explained I wanted to be an Army Ranger and get started as soon as possible. Within two weeks I began a four-year enlistment that would end twenty years later.

To be an Army Ranger required assimilation into a Spartan lifestyle and commitment to a two-year odyssey of training. Typically, Army Rangers volunteered a minimum of four times to continue with sequential phases of training. First, you had to volunteer to join the Army and then successfully pass Basic Training and Advanced Individual Training. Second, you had to volunteer for and pass the U.S. Army Airborne School at Fort Benning, Georgia. Third, you had to volunteer to attend the Ranger Indoctrination Program and accept assignment within the 75th Ranger Regiment. Fourth, you had to volunteer for and successfully pass the U.S. Army Ranger School. If a candidate failed any phase of training, for any reason, he was terminated and subject to worldwide assignment at the needs of the Army. As a leader these four phases of training were mandatory. Upon completion you had earned your Black Beret, black and gold Ranger tab and the opportunity to serve in the 75th Ranger Regiment.

All Rangers were imbued with a "never fail" and "complete the mission" ethos. This included an understood mandate to "never leave a fallen comrade."

RANGER CREED

<u>R</u>ecognizing that I volunteered as a Ranger. Fully knowing the hazards of my chosen profession. I will always endeavor to uphold the prestige, honor and high Esprit de Corps of my Ranger Regiment.

<u>A</u>cknowledging the fact that a Ranger is a more elite soldier who arrives at the cutting edge of battle by land, sea or air. I accept the fact that as a Ranger my country expects me to move further, faster and to fight harder than any other soldier.

<u>N</u>ever shall I fail my comrades. I will always keep myself mentally alert, physically strong and morally straight. I will shoulder more of the task, whatever it may be, one hundred percent and then some.

<u>G</u>allantly will I show the world that I am a specially selected and well-trained soldier. My courtesy to superior officers, neatness of dress, and care of equipment shall set the example for others to follow.

<u>E</u>nergetically will I meet the enemies of my country. I shall defeat them on the field of battle. For I am better trained and will fight with all my might. Surrender is not a Ranger word. I will never leave a fallen comrade to fall into the hands of the enemy and under no circumstances will I ever embarrass my country.

<u>R</u>eadily will I display the intestinal fortitude required to fight on to the Ranger objective and complete the mission, though I be the lone survivor. Rangers lead the way!

During my service in the 75th Ranger Regiment I had the opportunity to work with some of the best soldiers, sailors, airman and marines the United States military had to offer. In the world of joint service Special Operations, the best soldiers from all services stepped forward to participate in an unknown world. This was the 'dark side' of military operations and unseen by those on the outside.

Our training was conducted across the United States and around the world in locations to include Panama, Haiti, Cuba, Puerto Rico, Jordan, Thailand, Egypt, England, France, and many others. This was realistic and dangerous training which regularly resulted in the injury and death of our comrades. This bond built during training was cemented in combat in Grenada, Panama, Haiti, Somalia, Afghanistan, and Iraq. This was a pact sealed in blood. No member of the joint team had any doubt that should they be lost in combat, the remainder of the team would come to their aide and recover them.

The Ranger mandate to "never leave a fallen comrade" and to "complete the mission" bled over into another unexpected arena—the effort to recover America's lost warriors. The United States government has endeavored to achieve the fullest possible accounting of Prisoners of War and Missing in Action left behind after the war in Southeast Asia. This included the POWs and MIAs missing in the countries of Laos and Cambodia.

This is a politically charged issue that has polarized the American public since Operation Homecoming in 1975. The United States government has made recovery of any POWs and MIAs a national priority. The families of the missing expected and anticipated long overdue results and Joint Task Force-Full Accounting (JTF-FA) was formed to accomplish this accountability mission. JTF-FA emplaced a mandatory prerequisite to ensure all Investigation Team Leaders were U.S. Army Rangers. These Ranger Team Leaders would spearhead the effort to recover the missing and the fallen. They understood their role to complete the mission—though they be the lone survivor.

*   *   *

My telephone rang and when I answered, I was greeted by my Army branch representative at the U.S. Army Personnel Command in Virginia. After a few pleasantries he asked if I would be interested in duty as a POW/MIA Team Leader. I was a bit surprised since I had little knowledge of the mission. I knew we attempted to recover our POWs and MIAs but had no idea of the scope of the operation. He explained that I would lead a team into Southeast Asia to locate and recover our missing POWs. My file was perfect for the job and he wanted to nominate me for the position. Assuming I passed an interview and approval process, I would be transferred to Hawaii to assume the post.

I was provided the name and telephone number of Lieutenant Colonel Mike Lerario, the Operations Director at Joint Task Force Full Accounting, at Camp H.M. Smith, Hawaii. I dialed the number and LTC Lerario answered the phone. He explained I fit the minimum requirements of a Ranger Qualified, Command Qualified, and Combat Arms Captain. He was also pleased that I was a graduate of the Long Range Surveillance Leaders Course which he had also attended. LTC Lerario further explained that Ranger officers were required to ensure the most tactically proficient and driven Team Leaders would ensure the completion of the mission. I fit the bill and we agreed to have me participate as an observer in one Joint Field Activity to Laos to assess if I would be offered the job.

*   *   *

Never Leave a Fallen Comrade

On 8 May 2000, I departed for Hawaii and a new challenge that would be unlike any that I had experienced to this point in my career. I had been a small child during the late 1960's but I remember sitting on my father's lap and watching the news. I have vivid memories of film clips of fighting soldiers and a rather disturbing image of a nude peace activist standing on a podium and talking into a microphone to the crowd. My Dad did not want me to watch that part so he changed the channel.

It was this era that shaped much of my awareness of patriotism and service to my country. I distinctly remember sitting in the front passenger seat of our old blue Ford station wagon and making a comment that I did not want to go to war. My father sternly counseled me that if my country called then it was my duty to serve. From that point on I never questioned the idea of duty or service to my country. It now seems ironic that thirty-five years later I would be going back to those same jungles I had seen on the television. I would search for the same soldiers that had formed those images and shaped much of my life.

I arrived at the Honolulu International Airport with my wife, rented a car and drove to downtown Honolulu to the Waikiki Beach area. I checked into the Hilton Hawaiian Village and walked around a bit to get a sense of my surroundings. This was a luxurious tourist setting positioned right on the beach. It was laced with a lush tropical island flare that any tourist would expect to see. Fountains filled with coy and tropical fish, flamingos, ducks and geese, and open air restaurants and bars were everywhere. At the Rainbow Lanai you could have a meal and a glass of wine while sitting next to a rock pool with ducks and geese swimming over tropical fish. This open air café teased your senses and provided a vista of the bright blue waters rolling into Waikiki Beach.

August 10, 1990, U.S. Public Law 101-355, designated the POW/MIA flag - *"as the symbol of our Nation's concern and commitment to resolving as fully as possible the fates of Americans still prisoner, missing and unaccounted for in Southeast Asia, thus ending the uncertainty for their families and the Nation."*

Joint Task Force-Full Accounting (JTF-FA) was located about eight miles to the west atop a ridgeline overlooking the Pearl Harbor Memorial. This area was called Halawa (pronounced Halava) Heights—home to the Pacific Command (PACOM) Headquarters and JTF-FA. The JTF-FA building was located just inside the main gate and to the right. It was an austere, sand- colored building with no windows other than the front door. I found parking far down a hill, trekked to the building, and went up a stairwell to the third floor. There I used a telephone located by a keypad cipher lock to have someone let me through the door.

The door popped open and I was greeted by a sailor in his white uniform. He escorted me to a large open office space with many desks and introduced my future team members that were present. They were a mixture of services to include Army, Marine Corps and Air Force. It was a cross-section of fourteen intelligence analysts and Lao linguists, twelve males and two females. They would comprise the backbone of the team for the next few years. I would learn to trust and depend upon each one of them.

The outgoing Lao Team Leader was Major Paul Sarat, an Army Infantry Officer. He was passionate regarding the POW/MIA issue and militant in his desire to bring the missing home. He was focused and adamant that his techniques were the effective avenue to success.

Marine Gunnery Sergeant Carabello was the Team Sergeant and an Intelligence Analyst. He had been on the team for a period of years and had extensive experience in Laos. He would be my right-hand man for the first half of my tour.

Master Sergeant Pat Clifford, was an Air Force analyst who had been with the team for the past two years. He was a good analyst, focused on the mission, and reliable. His Lao time had been limited until this point.

Sergeant First Class Becky Sorrel was an Army Analyst who had yet to deploy with the Investigation Element (IE). She worked hard to be ready for her turn in Laos. She was a career soldier.

Sergeant Ryan Henson was a Marine with exceptional potential. He was so talented that he was never truly challenged. Unfortunately, he was waiting for his first opportunity to depart the military and start his life back home in Texas.

Air Force Sergeant Tommy Phisayavong was of Lao descent and the Investigation Element linguist. He was very adept at his job and the Lao liked him.

(Left to right) MSgt Danny Brodeur, SSgt Brown, SFC Sun, MSgt Tui Phosarath, SGT Victoria Watson, Unknown Augmenteur, MSG Collins, SFC Beurk Keomanivong, Gunnery Sergeant Kenkeo Chantakhot, SSG Nakiengchanh, and SSgt Martin.

The Lao Team included the linguists who translated diplomatic documents to and from English and Lao. They also provided the linguist capability to the Excavation Teams attempting to recover remains. Our linguist team was experienced and a critical asset to the POW/MIA recovery mission. TSgt Jack Kenkeo, MSgt Sengphet (Tui) Phosarath,

SFC Beurk Keomanivong, SFC Savoeung Sun, SSG Somdeth Nakhiengchanh, MSgt Danny Brodeur, SSgt Sirot Martin, SGT Victroia Watson, and SGT Boupha were extremely proficient at their linguist mission. They provided a wealth of cultural and country knowledge and effectively negotiated for both the Investigation and Excavation Elements as they dealt with the Lao and Cambodian officials. Their role was utterly invaluable and countless families owe them a debt of gratitude. Without them, nothing would have been accomplished. Replacements could be found for all job specialties—except for the linguists.

The Lao government required a complete family history of potential U.S. military Lao linguists be submitted for approval. This packet would be screened to ensure the linguists family history did not include a link to elements perceived as a threat to the Lao government. This was an area of great debate that I had always deemed as unacceptable—a standing requirement to force a U.S. military member to surrender their entire family history to a communist government. This invited the opportunity for the Lao government to influence our linguists with the threat of repercussions against their families still in Laos. I was informed this was a "voluntary" release of information, but if the information were not supplied, they would lose their job and be transferred.

It was interesting to note that JTF-FA was a Joint Command, which meant all services would be involved. Also, it had been decided that the manning commitment from each service would be proportional to the service's percentage of the number of POW/MIAs missing in Southeast Asia. Therefore, the majority were Air Force, followed by Army, Marine Corp and Navy.

During the next week, I gained an introduction into the operations of JTF-FA and met the other people who ran the unit. It was a very close-knit organization of military and civilian employees bound by a special mission to account for the missing. The priority was to investigate any possibility of a POW/MIA still alive in Southeast Asia: to find them, repatriate them and get them home. Second in priority was to locate the remains of servicemen who had died and were never recovered. We needed to find their remains, repatriate them to U.S. custody, confirm their identity, and return them to their families.

During my first week, I tried to take in as much information as possible, but this was an environment in which I had no prior experience. The interrelationships of staff offices and their ties to POW/MIA civilian organizations would take some time to appreciate. Even where relationships were clear-cut, it was hard to gauge the impact, influence, and fervor of organizations and personalities. Some individuals were very amicable and some relationships were very tenuous.

It was during this time that I met Bill Forsyth, the Laos intelligence analyst. Bill was a big and confident man with a pleasant personality. He would turn out to be my most valued and relied upon confidant. He was the hub of all investigation and recovery operations in Laos and he knew each case in minute detail.

One afternoon, I had just returned to my hotel room from a run on the beach when I received a phone call. A voice on the other end requested I come to a place called 'Stony Beach' for a briefing on the POW/MIA issue. It seemed strange since I had no idea who they were or what they were talking about. I called LTC Mike Lerario who said it was no problem, but he encouraged me to be *careful*. As I drove to Hickam Air Force Base for the briefing, I felt I was the only one who had no idea what the hell was going on. I went through the main gate of Hickam AFB and followed the directions. Manicured streets lined with beautiful draping palm trees passed on both sides. I found the hangar, parked my car, and entered through a side door.

Once inside, I met the men of Stony Beach. This was a group of Defense Intelligence analysts and debriefers dedicated to the POW/MIA recovery issue. I had no prior knowledge of their importance and they explained their organizational charter. Their post Vietnam War focus had been to interview Lao refugees in Thai refugee camps to gain information on missing servicemen.

Under pressure from the families of the missing, these debriefers had been brought into an active interview role in conjunction with JTF-FA operations. The men of Stony Beach argued that JTF-FA analysts, interviewers, and linguists, did not provide the results the families expected. This briefing was very informative and I had learned a great deal. I found my way out and returned to the hotel.

JTF-FA operations personnel later explained that this brief was an attempt to meet the new Team Leader (me) and ensure I was aware of their perspective to the POW/MIA issue. This was likely a result of the previous Joint Field Activity (JFA) to Laos in April.

During that April JFA, a Stony Beach debriefer was informed there would be no room for him on the plane. The Lao allowed a maximum of forty personnel on each JFA and the debriefer was deemed non-critical. The current Team Leader had determined that another team member was more important to the mission and the debriefer would have to wait until the next trip.

Army Brigadier General Harry Axson, the JTF-FA Commanding General rescinded the Team Leader's decision. The debriefer was then allowed to accompany the team. During the Joint Field Activity, the debriefer accused the Team Leader of impeding his ability to have access to witnesses and conduct interviews. That incident marked the beginning of a turf war. I would watch the dynamics of this struggle for the next three years and attempt to accommodate Stony Beach while ensuring the families got the best possible investigation of their missing loved ones.

I worked very closely and amicably with "Chief," the Army Chief Warrant Officer who often worked with my team. Chief and I worked together to placate the issue and keep any friction between ourselves. We worked well together and disagreed occasionally—okay, often. These arguments and differences of opinions were always worked out at our level and out of the sight of our superiors. The issue remained placated until my third year when Chief was replaced by two other debriefers—DB1 and DB2. DB1 and DB2 stretched my patience terribly.

I tried hard to encourage them to be part of the team and be receptive to constructive input. Regardless, it was a very strained relationship. No matter how patient I was, or how much advice I would try to give, they were stubborn and refused to consider doing things another way. For example, they insisted they conduct their interviews in the absence of JTF-FA personnel. I believe they felt this would limit distractions and make them the focal point.

My team tried to explain that they should attempt to capitalize on relationships with the Lao officials that we had developed. A critical component of gaining information from a witness was the Lao official's assurances that cooperation was permitted. Without this assurance and permission we would get no useful information. Often, Lao officials would take me to the side and tell me how frustrated they were with the interview techniques of DB1 and DB2. They were also irritated by the debriefers' off-duty discussions with local citizens at restaurants and on the streets.

The Lao knew DB1, in particular, was continuously trying to gather behind the scenes information. They talked to me often about trying to rein him in. In the end, it just would not sink in to the debriefers to adopt a participative tone and I felt they actually damaged relationships and limited the success of specific investigations. I informed my Chain of Command of this problem. The situation presented a dilemma. A political decision had brought Stony Beach into the fold and in addition, the organization was supported by the DPMO and American League of Families. The American League of Families was a powerful lobbying group of family members imploring the U.S. Government to bring their family members home. They had direct lobbying influence on the Defense POW/MIA Office (DPMO). Stony Beach worked for the DPMO.

In my opinion, this was a point where well-meaning families had influenced a poor decision. The Lao farmer, hunter, or ex-soldier was not a sophisticated person. He lived in a simple rural environment and had a distrust of westerners and any person from outside his immediate community. The leading and manipulative interview technique of the debriefers was easy to recognize. Witnesses often threw up walls of protection for self-preservation.

The Stony Beach debriefers and the JTF-FA Investigation Element may have disagreed on the techniques, but we were both after the truth of what had happened to our POWs and MIAs. Our combined results during that period were exceptional.

The relationship between the Lao and U.S. Teams was also tempered with mutual tentative and strained cooperation. From the U.S. standpoint, the effort to recover servicemen and return them to their families was a simple concept. The Lao did not disagree on this humanitarian effort but used this U.S. national priority as an opportunity to further their own nation-building efforts. This effort included reconstruction, economic investment, and world community visibility and recognition. Therefore, fluctuating levels of cooperation were directly linked to U.S. commitments to investments in Lao civic projects. The focal point of all diplomatic efforts relating to the POW/MIA effort was the Commander of JTF-FA. Therefore, U.S. commitment was easily regulated to maximize our operations. First and foremost the Lao wanted compensation. Negotiations for vehicles, staff members, aircraft usage hours, and country over-flight fees, all boiled down to that same point—compensation.

The Lao would easily make over a million U.S. dollars on each trip. They employed an entire team of government officials to mirror our team and theoretically enable our operations. In true Lao fashion, within a culturally accepted system of graft, they skimmed the profits from coordination and compensation to the Lao workers and local officials. This United States national priority had become a Lao 'cash cow.' To regulate the progress of Investigation and Recovery operations was definitely to the Lao government's advantage.

JTF-FA walked the line between politics and compensation ensuring the most productive climate existed between the Lao and U.S. teams. This climate, combined with the political pressure of POW/MIA lobbying groups to bring back results, directly determined success and failure of investigations and recoveries in Laos.

This dynamic required an understanding of multiple organizations and the political forces which pulled their strings. At the top was the Defense Prisoner of War/Missing Personnel Office (DPMO) under which three other organizations operated: Joint Task Force-Full Accounting, Central Identification Laboratory Hawaii, and Stony Beach.

The DPMO had the mission to lead the national effort to account for personnel missing as the result of hostile action and establish the most favorable conditions to recover those who become isolated in harm's way.

JTF-FA was formed in 1992 in response to political pressure to provide the fullest possible accounting of servicemen lost in Southeast Asia and it replaced the Joint Casualty Resolution Center. The Joint Casualty Resolution Center had been formed in 1973 to lead U.S. Government POW/MIA recovery efforts in Southeast Asia.

These military organizations were very aware of the political pressure and influence induced by the American League of Families and the National Alliance of Families. Both of these organizations had direct political influence the affected recovery operations.

The Central Identification Laboratory in Hawaii has the worldwide mission to recover remains of servicemen lost in all wars or conflicts. Their mission is far reaching and focused on the recovery of remains, positive identification and subsequent return of the servicemen to their families.

In 2001, there were still forty-six aircraft remaining undiscovered in Laos. Over eighty previously discovered sites presented a seven to ten year backlog on the excavation list. This excavation waiting list was a point in the system where a family or organization could pressure a case up the list. This would be at the expense of other families waiting patiently for their cases to be excavated.

To comprehend the challenges of the POW/MIA recovery effort in Southeast Asia required a basic understanding of how the Vietnam War ended. During the Vietnam War, the North Vietnamese had entered Laos using a series of roads and trails to ferry troops and supplies towards the south. This network was termed the Ho Chi Minh trail. To counter this threat,

American forces staged from Thailand, South Vietnam, and the South China Sea, and conducted extensive air strikes throughout Laos. The Americans also sent Special Forces reconnaissance teams and CIA operatives into Laos and Cambodia. These teams had the mission to report on enemy movements along the Ho Chi Minh Trail and to organize a guerilla army by utilizing the Hmong hill tribes. The Hmong hill tribes of Laos were fiercely independent and historically had fought against the Vietnamese.

Most Americans are not familiar with the geography of Southeast Asia. (Laos Website)

During the Vietnam War, over six-hundred American POWs were known to have been taken captive by the Pathet Lao. Many of them were then taken to the Houaphan region in northern Laos. There they were kept in a network of caves where they were easily guarded and secured from rescue.

No POW/MIA was ever released from Laos, even during Operation Homecoming in 1973. None of the known POWs was included in the list of repatriated POWs. Henry Kissinger had negotiated a deal with the Vietnamese to pay over $3 billion in reparations. It was made clear that POWs in Laos would not be made part of this deal. It was a separate issue and they would be released separately.

Again, no POW known to be in Laos with the Pathet Lao was *ever* released. Only two had ever escaped alive. One was Dieter Dengler, shot down February 2, 1965, and the other was Navy Lieutenant Charles Klussman, shot down on June 2, 1964. All others have remained unaccounted for and that drives the U.S. efforts to bring home the missing.

*   *   *

Chapter 2
Land of a Million Elephants

My first trip to Laos would begin a sequence of Joint Field Activities where success or failure directly affected the lives of many families back home. Each Investigation Element was entrusted with the hopes of these families to bring home their missing servicemen from Laos and Cambodia. I understood this charge and it was both empowering and sobering. Someday I would have to look those family members in the eye and answer for the work we had done for them.

On deployment day the team assembled at Hickham Air Force Base along with three Excavation Teams. The Excavation Teams would dig sites previously identified by the Investigation Element and we would continue to investigate. Family members accompanied the teams to have a last few minutes to say goodbye before we loaded the plane.

I had taken the opportunity to bring my wife to Honolulu with me to get a chance to enjoy the island together for a week. Now I was off to Southeast Asia and she was off to the Reserve Officer Training Corp Basic Camp at Fort Knox, Kentucky. In August, we would meet in Iowa and move to Hawaii together. For now we went in separate directions.

The team said our long goodbyes and boarded a charter flight which would carry us through Guam and on to Pattaya, Thailand. That was where Detachment 1 of JTF-FA facilitated the movement of men and supplies in and out of Vietnam, Laos, and Cambodia.

*   *   *

We arrived at the airport in Thailand and took a forty-minute bus ride Pattaya. We checked into a hotel JTF-FA habitually used to house our teams. Layovers of 36 to 72 hours were common as we attempted to align commercial and military flights into Thailand with military flights into Laos, Cambodia, and Vietnam. Flights into Laos had to be via C-130 and were flown by National Guard crews on temporary duty in the region. These Vietnam era cargo planes were only semi-reliable and kept our missions on schedule only half of the time. This made it a challenge to fly into Thailand, trans-load onto the C-130s, and continue on our way to Laos.

View from the hotel room in Pattaya, Thailand

Pattaya was an exotic location famous for its adult playground. It was rumored Pattaya was run by the Russian mafia and they gleaned the profits. It was a maze of bars, bar girls, massage parlors, and the exotic hustle and bustle of a venue set to attract the European tourist. It also had an endless supply of cheap, brand name, counterfeit clothing. This was where we bought clothes to be ruined in the jungles during each trip to Laos.

During one of these shopping sprees I was walking down a street and bar girls called out, "Hey sexy—buy me drink?" I was feeling pretty good about myself as I continued on my way. I paused and looked up at the sign which arched over the entrance of the street. In big and bold letters it read, "*Boy's Town.*" I asked some of the other guys what that meant. They said it was the transvestite part of the bar district. I didn't feel too sexy after that.

We boarded our C-130 and took a direct two-hour flight route to the capital city of Vientiane on the Mekong River. Once on the ground we taxied to a remote corner of the tarmac away from the commercial air terminal. We stepped off the airplane into a baking sun and air heavy with humidity. This was hot even for Hawaii and similar to the mid-west on a very hot and humid summer day. We found a bit of shade under the wing of the plane and waited while our passports were collected and taken to the customs agents for stamping. Our Lao officials then arrived in two Pajero sport utility vehicles and stepped out to greet us. From that point forward we never went anywhere without a Lao official being present. The Air Force Load Master then opened the back ramp of the C130 and we trans-loaded equipment to a waiting MI-17 Soviet helicopter that would ferry us deeper into the country.

Depending on the province in which we would conducting our investigations, the team would stay at either a small rustic inn or at one of the established base camps. There were exceptions to this rule based on practical logistical requirements to live at or near a remote site.

There were two main options for a base camp—Ban (village) Alang and Ban Ta-oy Base Camps. Ban Alang Base Camp was in Savannakhet Province, Laos. It had been built in close proximity to a large number of discovered sites already on the excavation list. This allowed quick access to the area and a tidy place for the Lao officials to keep the Americans in a tight and secure compound. The Lao were genuinely concerned with our safety and they did not want us randomly mixing with the local population.

Ban Alang Base Camp

In 2002, a second base camp was established at Ban Ta-Oy, Salavan Province. It was originally scheduled to be constructed in Salavan City. My team had wrestled with the unpredictable weather patterns in this area for the previous two years. Therefore, upon my team's recommendation, the site was relocated east of the mountain range separating Salavan City from the eastern border areas. This was where most sites in Salavan and Xekong provinces were located.

Each base camp had a similar set up of small rows of tents on concrete pads and walkways to the latrines, showers, common cooking area, weights, helipads and a small diner. The diner had Lao cooks who would make your basic three meals each day as long as you ordered from a predetermined and unchanging menu. This menu was supported by the vegetables, meat, and eggs purchased from the local villages. We often negotiated with the cooks for alternatives to the menu. For example, if we provided our own pancake mix and syrup, the diner would make it for us but still charge us. For me, every day was six scrambled eggs and four pancakes for breakfast. After that I could fend for myself out of a box of favorites I brought with on each trip.

The hot water for the shower came from gravity feed fifty-gallon drums of non-potable water treated with bleach. It was heated by a propane burner. Each morning a Lao worker would light the flame for morning showers. During the day the sun would heat the black painted barrels for the evening showers. Bottled water was used for teeth brushing and shaving.

The latrines consisted of a concrete block structure with five stalls fitted with western style commodes. A single yellow light bulb hovered on a string above your head. The yellow bulb was less of an attractant to the flying insects during the nighttime hours. There was no running water. Therefore, you would have to stop and fill a three gallon bucket of water at a spigot outside. Then carry your bucket into a stall with you. After you did your "business," you would flush it down with your bucket of water.

The plastic plumbing would route the waste out to the river behind the camp.

Squirrels operating out of Ta-oy Base Camp.

There were almost always two MI-17 and four AS-350 "Squirrel" helicopters parked at the camps. These were primarily our only mode of travel as ground vehicle travel was highly discouraged for multiple reasons. One reason being the terrible quality of the pothole ridden roads. These roads extended travel times, caused vehicle breakdown, and increased the likelihood of an injury to a team member. Another reason to avoid the roads was the Lao and Vietnamese driver's free-for-all mentality of high speeds and a lack of awareness of driving lanes. That combined with the poor road conditions made travel on the roads extremely dangerous.

The lack of a developed road system made timely access to most areas available only by helicopter. We used a contract air company called Lao West Coast which was run by a company called Helicopters New Zealand. All of the pilots were Kiwi or Aussie. They made their living supporting the mining and oil exploration companies in the region. Their other big contract was to support the U.S. POW/MIA effort. Their experience and skill was honed from many years and thousands of flight hours as bush pilots. On many occasions, they would display their flying skills as they inserted and extracted us from small openings in the jungle canopy. It was truly amazing what they could do. Time and again they saved our butts.

Although life in the base camps provided a feeling of relative security, moving around after dark could be high adventure. In the grass one could encounter bamboo vipers and cobra snakes along with scorpions. It was always best to make a beeline for a sidewalk and stay out of the grass. During the monsoon season these critters also had a bad habit of entering any opening in the tent flaps to find a dry place. When you woke up in the morning or late at night to go to the latrine, you had to survey the tent floor with a flashlight to ensure nothing lurked there. You *never* put on your boots or clothes without shaking them out first. You had to ensure nothing had taken up residence in there. Only once did I have a snake get into my tent. It was about eighteen inches long and I beat it to death with a boot.

Life in the base camps during the rainy season.

The other lurking threat waiting to attack you was the "funk," the unexplainable overpowering of your immune system by invisible little critters found in the water, food, and air. Washing your hands, staying clean, and taking your anti-malarial prophylaxis was always foremost in your mind. The funk was a patient opponent and surfaced without warning. Individual team members came down with extremely painful flu-like symptoms. Also, intermittent cases of malaria affected both our team and our contracted pilots.

On my second trip to Laos the funk attacked me after eating dinner at the diner. I rolled around in agony for the next 48 hours. My body purged itself from both ends and finally the Doc knocked me out with a painkiller and Cipro cocktail. The Cipro killed all the bacteria in your intestinal tract and became

26

the medicine of choice. The funk was there and utterly unpredictable.

Accommodations at the Boulapha Base Camp.

Malaria was even sneakier due to its delayed reactions. We took Doxycycline daily and Primaquine for two weeks upon arrival back home. Supposedly, with this combination you were 99.9 percent safe from malaria. Unfortunately, we had two team members in two successive JFAs contract malaria. The evidence suggested that due to our busy and fluid schedule, team members would forget to take it regularly. After a lapse, they would double the dosage in an attempt to make up for the missed days. This was not an effective approach and allowed the parasites the opportunity to infect the blood stream. It would not be until we returned to Hawaii that the individual came down with cold and flu symptoms and ended up in the hospital. After the second case, I charged the team medic with the responsibility of ensuring that each team member took their meds everyday while in Laos. He personally went from team member to team member and directed them to place the medication in their mouth while he watched.

Ta-oy Base Camp, Laos.

The inns were better for our investigations operations. They allowed us to have complete autonomy to work our investigation schedules with our Lao counterparts. The officials were always more on guard in the base camps because their boss was sure to be there. That meant a less congenial atmosphere and our investigation flexibility could be limited.

There were other political repercussions of co-locating the Investigation Element with the Recovery Elements at the Base

Camps. The Recovery Elements had their own challenges of negotiating with Lao government and local officials to establish the resources to perform excavations. This often involved negotiation of access to the village area, the number of workers to be hired, the length of the excavation period, and payment of monies. This was a tenuous set of negotiations and the RE Team Leaders had continuous challenges to control theft and assure their workforce came to work. Due to this friction with the officials the IE preferred to stage their operations from a site separate from the base camp.

*   *   *

On this first Joint Field Activity, our destination was Houaphan Province located in the northeastern part of Laos and adjacent to Vietnam. It was the communist bastion from which the current regime had fought during the Vietnam War. The area had an extensive system of caves in the Limestone Mountains. This provided relative safety from the continuous American bombing along the Ho Chi Min trail. It was also a location where numerous American aircraft had been shot down and numerous POWs and MIAs were reported to have been seen alive during the war.

Xam Nua sported a concrete runway that received weekly flights from Vientiane and we parked our aircraft next to rows of fifty gallon fuel drums that had been delivered by trucks before our arrival. We loaded a flatbed truck and then bounced down a gravel road past rustic houses and flooded rice fields into the town.

We took up residence in a government run hotel across from the district military headquarters and prepared to begin work the next day. An interesting development occurred on the first night. At 5 p.m. the government public address system began blasting music and announcements over a set of loudspeakers. The message said, "Work hard, be good, and good things will come to you." They played these messages every morning and night and considering the primitive state of the city and countryside it was probably a necessity for the people.

Conditions were very poor and this was considered to be a developed area. It was a combination of dirt, gravel and paved roads with heavy traffic from every form of vehicle, animal,

Xam Nua Airport, Houaphan Province, Laos.

bicycle, and motorcycle transportation you could think of. This constant flow of traffic and lack of clean paved roads created a constant cloud of dust that got into everything.

We began our investigations in the hills bordering Vietnam where bombing of the Ho Chi Min trail during the war had resulted in many aircraft losses in the nearby mountains. This was also the area where the Hmong hill tribes, who gained a ferocious reputation while fighting with the Green Berets, were located. After the war, the Lao government attempted to exterminate the Hmong and drove them into the remote hills to hide. They are still there now and living in the most primitive conditions imaginable. They have little contact with the outside world and rarely leave.

The men of the Hmong did most of the hunting and foraging for food and the trading of goods with neighboring villages. The women tended to the family, livestock, and rice paddies. It was a communal effort and villages often bristled with the energy of daily rural activities.

Usually, when we landed in a village people would run at us from all directions to see what the big commotion was. To have a helicopter land with white foreigners was a big event not to be missed. As the crowd congregated around the Squirrel, which almost always arrived first, they would stare in awe at the raw power and size of the MI-17 as it came into view a few minutes behind. The MI-17 could generate extreme rotor wash and blow down rice fields, take off the roofs of village huts, and send cattle and water buffalo stampeding through the fields.

A Hmong family in traditional hand-woven dress clothes.

The buffalo became a major concern for the helicopters. If the herd scattered during our landings, they would do anything to get back to each other. That included charging right through the tail booms of the helicopters. I had seen this happen with the Squirrel and luckily it did not seriously damage the tail boom.

The walk to the village was an opportunity to meet and greet the people. We enjoyed "rock star" status and almost all older women and men would want to shake our hands. "Sabaidi" (saw-by-dee) was the common greeting and one of the few Hmong words I would ever learn. I had tried other words but the linguists told me to stop talking before I offended someone by saying the wrong thing.

A Lao village in Xiangkhoang Province.

The older women usually wore a sarong (wrap around skirt), thong sandals, and very often no shirt. Their skin had a leathery appearance from years of sun exposure. They would greet you with a chewing tobacco or betel smile of brown teeth and blackish-brown spittle on their lips. This was a proud people, always very genuine, and they seemed so happy. They were detached from any concern of political or world events and were concerned only with the life in their immediate community.

Khammouan Province in central Laos.

The building style varied greatly from north to south across the different regions and tribal areas. From Houaphan to Salavan Provinces the general style was a house on strong beam uprights with either plank or split bamboo flooring. This style utilized grass thatch roofs to route the rains off the sides of the huts. The split bamboo flooring did not generate confidence to bigger western men who entered the huts during interviews. The floor would bounce and strain but not once did I see it give way. Split bamboo is very stringy and therefore very strong.

The building style in Attapu and Xekong provinces was unique. I would describe it as the large oval lodge style housing of American Indians in the northeastern United States. These houses were built with heavy timbered uprights, plank flooring, and a large center beam down the middle and length of the structure. Walls of woven bamboo would then make separate family units. The inside of these houses were very dark and blackened by soot from years of interior cooking fires. Occasionally, I would lay back inside the chief's lodge while we waited for him to come in from the surrounding fields. As my eyes wandered around the room, I would marvel at this snapshot of their culture. I would attempt to frame in my mind the vision of the soot-covered fishing nets, crossbows for hunting, a rifle used to protect the village from prowling tigers, and artifacts from the war found in the jungle.

*   *   *

My trip as an observer into Laos proved to be a painful experience. I intended to learn everything possible from my predecessor but friction began early on in the deployment. It became apparent that a wall of secrecy existed between the augmenters and existing members of the team. This exclusion included a Special Forces medic named Doc McCaughey and "Chief," the Stony Beach interviewer.

The karsts of Khammouan Province.

I questioned why Sergeant Henson was permitted to get an orange hair dye job in Thailand and the core members of the team spent their deployment socializing. Then during a short trek up a steep hill on a hot day, two members of the team went down with heat exhaustion. They could not complete the mission. I cast a questioning eye at this situation. It was explained to me that maximum latitude was given for after hours conduct. The expectation was that each team member would be able to deliver on mission days. Now two team members were collapsed on the side of the trail. It was obvious this did not equate to completion of any mission.

It was not my place, as an observer, to question the climate of the team. However, when the team climate became hostile and safety became an issue, I just could not help myself. I would not stand for an intoxicated team member doing a "Teen

Wolf" imitation by standing up and "surfing" in the MI-17 during flight. Chief, Doc McCaughey, and I gradually gravitated together. We spent many hours discussing the dynamics we were experiencing. Another reason for our being shunned came to light later in the JFA.

It was firmly against U.S. policy to pay any witness or official for possible POW/MIA remains (bones) or personal items such as rings, watches, Identification Tags or Cards, etc. This non-compensation policy did not work well in Laos. Laos was a poor country and everything had value. If a witness had a ring, he expected to be paid for it. Therefore, possible evidence may be discovered during an investigation but no effective mechanism existed, other than goodwill, to retrieve it.

Previous frustrated Team Leaders (not all Team Leaders) had developed a way around this situation where they would pad the numbers of workers or witnesses tallied for each JFA. This was the unofficial means of officially paying the Lao government for their support. For example, if I hired ten workers for a day, each worker would receive twenty-five dollars. If a Team Leader wanted to procure an item or gain support from the village chief, he could negotiate the number of workers required for a task. The task may not even exist. Or, you could hire twenty-five workers, for a five-worker job, and only five workers would show up. Either way the Lao got their money. As a Team Leader you could work these deals within a very fuzzy and gray ethical line. The reality was only two dollars were paid to the workers and the Lao government pocketed the rest. There was no telling at what level the funds were skimmed or disbursed. This was payable at the end of each JFA. JTF-FA paid an inclusive tally through to the government in one final bill.

The exclusion of the augmenters was an effort to shield us from the deals aggressively being worked. Whatever deals had been negotiated during past JFA's needed to be completed during this trip. I would inherit any left behind on the next JFA.

*   *   *

On our first investigation, we stopped at a remote Hmong village nestled amongst thickly forested mountains. We landed alongside a nearby rice field, jumped from stone to stone across a creek, and arrived in the village. The Hmong villagers seemed very pleased to see us.

Hmong village in Houaphan province.

We had delayed our visit to this village until a local official had delivered an official notification letter to the village chief of our pending arrival. The Lao national officials were concerned that without prior coordination they could not guarantee our safety. This seemed a prudent procedure after two young village men became alarmed at our presence in their village. They had just returned from the jungle carrying antique long barreled hunting rifles. Another villager waved to the young men and they seemed relieved.

We removed our boots at the bottom of a ladder, climbed up and ducked into a shallow doorway and into the chief's hut. There we found our way to a space in a circle as we sat cross-legged and faced the center. After some introductions, the interview of the village chief ensued. Tommy began with a questioning routine to gather information on the age of the village, where the villagers went during the war years, and how far they would hunt and fish from the village now. Then it focused on what they had found in the surrounding jungle

The village chief told us about an airplane crash in the mountains nearby. We had a historical database of lost aircraft and this did not fit. Therefore it was determined the crash site warranted an inspection to ensure it did not involve a missing crew. It was possible the crash site involved a "Scope Loss." A Scope Loss involved an aircraft that was tracked for a period of time on radar and then just dropped of the scope—never to return. The formal interview was over and the chief invited the group to toast this very special occasion.

His wife entered with a bottle of Lao Lao (rice moonshine) and a platter of small shot glasses. Also, a young man appeared carrying a Lao Hi crock (primitive beer equivalent). Lao Hi was made by pushing a gourd into the bottom of the crock and filling the remainder with rice to ferment. After the proper aging process it would be consumed. Long reed straws were pushed past the rice and into the center of the gourd that served as a strainer. Then the crock was filled to the brim with water. Drinking Lao Hi was a social occasion and each straw was expected to be manned by someone at the gathering. It could be a competition to see who could drink the most. It could also be a battle of wills to act like you were drinking in the hopes the other person would imbibe more than his share. There was considerable peer pressure as everyone in the room watched. Often the water level would not move while four people on the straws acted like they were sucking as hard as they could.

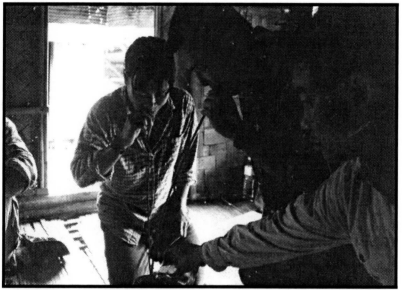

Boupha at the Lao hi gourd as Tommy pours water in the top.

The investigation day ground to a halt with a raucous party in the village chief's hut. Ryan Henson stood in the middle of the room, with his mussed red hair, wildly strumming his air guitar in a windmill motion and singing a rendition of Billy Idol's "White Wedding." The villagers were wildly entertained and enjoying the occasion.

The Investigation Element had found success through being social with the Lao officials and villagers. They firmly believed this was the mechanism to break down barriers to gather information. It was explained that in the past, information and cooperation was not readily offered. Only relationships built during a carefree social approach had paid dividends.

View from the LZ - the mountains of northern Laos.

The next day we loaded into the Lao West Coast AS-350 helicopter referred to as the 'Squirrel' and shuttled to the mountaintop landing zone. We stepped off the skid of the aircraft onto the pointed peak of the mountain. From this vista you could see far across the mountains in all directions. A Lao villager then moved us down the mountain on a steep trail which he cut with a machete. In a single file we went down through the thick brush. Flies, bees and gnats tried their best to get at any exposed skin. After about forty minutes we came upon the wreckage of an airplane on the steep slope.

You could see the airplane had augured into the ground like a lawn dart—its green colored wings folded back onto itself. The engines had separated from the fuselage and rolled slightly back downhill. The heavier landing struts had propelled forward up the slope and broken into heavy cylindrical sections. We leaned our rucksacks against small trees to keep them from rolling down the hillside. Then we prepared to search the surrounding jungle. I moved with the team in a single lateral line (a line search) as we worked our way downhill. We picked through large pieces of wreckage in the very thick vegetation. We hoped to locate any piece of wreckage to specifically correlate the airplane in the database. That would tell us a history of the crash and if the crew was missing. We also searched for any piece of life-support equipment or piece of the ejection seat. Any of these items would indicate a crewmember was likely in the aircraft upon impact.

These searches were painful and grueling. The grass and thorn bushes cut at our exposed skin and the unrelenting heat sapped our strength. There is nothing like a bead of sweat running down the middle of your back, legs, or crack of the butt. In your mind there was no doubt a big leech was moving around inside your clothes.

Each crash site inspection offered the opportunity for injury. The sharp edges of metal, potential for unexploded ordnance, and environmental risks were always a threat. You never handled the wreckage with bare hands and you had to be careful of the unexpected. One of those valuable lessons was learned the hard way when four of us tried to roll over the engine. As we rolled it, a team member's glove got snagged by a protruding piece of metal. As the heavy engine started to roll it threatened to pull him over and then under the engine as it careened down the steep slope. Fortunately, his leather glove slipped off his hand. You had to be slow and deliberate during any crash site survey.

After we rolled the engine, I decided to continue searching down the slope. My theory was that the metal would roll down to the steep incline to the bottom. I clawed my way through thick vines and thorn bushes to the bottom. A search of the creek bed produced nothing of note. Then I fought my way back through the vegetation to get back up the hill. Just when I was getting close to the rucksacks, the team had started to move back to the landing zone. With my chest heaving, I put on my rucksack, and then started up. The team pressed the pace and I labored behind.

*   *   *

This had been my first crash site inspection and I learned a lot from the experience. Strange pieces of wreckage at a crash site would later in my tenure become readily identifiable. I would develop the ability to apply specific meaning to the metal parts within the wreckage field. I would also learn from experience that it took two full years, or six JFAs, to become a truly effective Team Leader in Laos. To know the terrain, officials, cases, wreckage, life support evidence, and search and interview techniques, required considerable on the job experience.

There was considerable debate as to whether a Team Leader from Vietnam could be effective in Laos. In Vietnam, there were three investigation teams with three associated Team Leaders. This meant that any one Team Leader would not have the time and latitude to intimately learn his cases. In Laos we had one Investigation Element and only one Team Leader.

There were individual Team Leaders who would not take the time to study their cases or area of responsibility. They felt their job was only to move the team of linguists and analysts safely in and about the country. I personally studied the fine detail of my cases to formulate the investigation plan.

Looking back, I would say a Team Leader without an intimate knowledge of his case load would deny an Investigation Element of a critical element to enhance success. Any Team Leader could be effective as long as his Team Sergeant and analysts were competent and well trained. That Team Leader could then sit in the background and watch the investigations unfold. To be a *truly effective* team required a complete and well-trained team—to include the Team Leader.

Working with VN and Lao witnesses to locate a crash site.

*　　*　　*

During that same JFA we visited a village, in Khammouan Province, Laos reported to have a crash site nearby. A team had reported this site years earlier and provided a detailed description of discovered evidence. A few years later another team visited the village and found no evidence of a crash site. Our mission was to revisit the village and resolve the discrepancy.

We arrived at the village and conducted a detailed interview of a small group of village elders. They confirmed there had been a crash site on the edge of the village but most of the wreckage had been scavenged and sold to metals buyers. A witness then led us to the edge of the village and we conducted a survey of the area.

During the search of the woodline I had intended to chop my way through a thicket. When I hit a piece of bamboo with my machete, I expected it to break and fall away. Instead, a shard of dried bamboo flew upward and embedded into my right eye. It was extremely painful and I could not open either eye. The Doc determined I had a scratched cornea and said it would go away. It turned out that something had shot in and under the white exterior of my eyeball. The pain persisted for weeks and a distinctive brown spot stained the white of my eye.

A year later I had a prescreening for corrective eye surgery. During the exam the Surgeon, Dr. Kevin Winkle, cut open my eye and surgically removed a piece of bamboo.

We searched diligently along the edge of a pasture and found small pieces of aluminum consistent with an aircraft. More searching revealed only other small pieces of unidentifiable wreckage with nothing conclusive. We could not correlate any incident or aircraft to the village and therefore ended the unsuccessful search. We knew when we left that we would be back to bring some resolution to this mystery.

*Typical landing zone for the Squirrel - hovering atop a karst
(piloted by Aussie Don Guthrie).*

We continued through this JFA and produced little of note. It had been a very difficult environment in which to gain experience. I did not feel I knew enough to be competent and would have to rely upon the advice of the other experienced Team Leaders and learn on the job.

*   *   *

Chapter 3
Into the Mist

Upon our return to Hawaii, we began training in earnest for our next trip to Laos. At JTF-FA we initiated a regimen of physical training, report writing, interview skills, and practice crash site surveys. Looking back, it was the minimum preparation of a team with untapped potential. At that time, I felt we were well prepared.

When I officially assumed my position as the Lao Team Leader, I asked for clear guidance from my superiors on issues I felt could get me in trouble. I especially wanted clear rules which governed what I could and could not do to recover remains and personal items. My opportunity would come at a pre-brief of the proposed investigation plan for my first JFA as Team Leader. The meeting was chaired by the Deputy Commander Colonel Kampsen. LTC Mike Lerario, Chief of the Operations Directorate, was also present.

After I had completed a short talk on the investigation plan, the Deputy Commander offered his suggestions and asked if there were any further questions. I voiced my concern that I did not have clear guidance on how to handle the matter of witness compensation and asked for his thoughts on the issue. There was a dramatic pause where the Deputy Commander looked uncomfortable and then irritated. He then looked at LTC Lerario and told him to get with me on the subject.

"Chief" was on my left and watched intently as he was also concerned about this topic—especially after our last trip to Laos. Chief and I did not agree on every topic, but he was always my honest broker. I could count on Chief to be a "straight shooter." I met with Lieutenant Colonel Lerario afterward, and he was clearly agitated that I had asked the question in that forum. I explained that I knew deals had been struck and a bad precedent set in Laos. I needed to know my boundaries. He replied that it was better to be "penny wise than pound foolish." Basically, if I could get something I was after for a few hundred dollars, and therefore save thousands of dollars in additional excavation or investigation costs, then it was my call.

*   *   *

Back in Laos we entered a valley heavily used by the North Vietnamese Army (NVA) to move men and materials into Laos. The Americans had bombed extensively for years and there were many aircraft shot down and still missing.

Hmong village tucked away in the mountains.

My team was tasked to investigate at all villages along the valley floor for possible crash sites in the area. At the main Area Village, we interviewed an "Area Chief" who said there were no crash sites nearby. He spoke for the seven villages, which inhabited the northern section of the valley—closest to the Vietnam border. The visit appeared to be a dry hole. Regardless, we made an appointment to return the next day to talk with a specific witness involving a report of POWs during the war. That evening, in the interim, the area chief asked around at six of his sub-villages about any crash sites in the area. One of those villages reported they had a crash site nearby.

When we arrived the next day, the chief took us to the site deep in the jungle. We walked up a streambed and then veered into a flat section of jungle covered in thick thorny vines. After a half-hour of searching the chief failed to find the site. We then hired ten villagers to find and clear the site for a survey the following day.

We returned the next day and villagers led us down a fresh cut trail to the crash site. They had cleared the vines away to reveal a crash crater about thirty feet across and three feet deep. There were cluster munitions spread throughout the site. The village chief informed us that villagers had been killed at this site by exploding ordinance while they salvaged aluminum to sell to metals buyers. Then the Lao officials and guides moved away from the site to avoid being killed in an explosion.

We tiptoed amongst the munitions and searched carefully. A surface search found nothing conclusive. Later, we took out the shovels and began to dig a little deeper to find evidence. I hit a good-sized piece of metal and used my shovel to try and pry it lose. It was large so I continued to dig deeper. Further down the edge of the metal slab I realized I was scraping the side of a 250 lb. bomb.

This site was a very early loss and had been missing since the early 1960's. It was heavily armed with 250 lb. bombs, cluster munitions, and 20 mm. cannon. That weapons load in itself correlated it to only one possible aircraft type - an A-1 Sky Raider. There was one lost A-1 Sky Raider left unaccounted for in our data base anywhere near this area. We had a likely correlation!

Circumstances of loss: (Courtesty POW/MIA Network.)
One of the aircraft launched from the HANCOCK was Douglas Aircraft's A1 Sky raider ("Spad"). On March 31, 1965, the pilot was launched on a bombing mission over Quang Binh Province, North Vietnam. During the mission near the city of Ron, the pilot was making bombing runs on a target, when, on his last pass, his aircraft was hit by anti-aircraft fire and crashed. Search and rescue efforts were unable to locate the site the pilot was listed Reported Deceased the same day.

This set of circumstances was very consistent with the evidence found at the crash site. Keith, our Life-Support Technician, uncovered a corroded parachute cable. This cable provided physical evidence that a crewmember was likely in the aircraft upon impact. This was our first significant find on my watch.

After our crash site survey we successfully located the witness with a reported knowledge of POW/MIAs in the area. This interview sequence was one of the biggest disappointments of my tenure in the POW/MIA arena.

The Douglas A-1 Sky raider carried a heavy assortment of ordnance and was used extensively in Southeast Asia. (Courtesy POW/MIA Net)

We sat down to interview an older Lao villager dressed in his old Pathet Lao Army uniform. Since Chief was the debriefer, he began with a series of questions that would have the witness describe his position and experience during the war years. During this exchange, the witness said he was a guard at a prison camp in northern Laos. He also claimed to have seen numerous Americans alive and in captivity during the war.

Chief generally took my suggestions but in this instance we disagreed on the next line of questioning. Chief wanted to get immediate descriptions of any prisoners the witness could remember. I wanted to stay more general and ask about years, locations, numbers and what happened to them. My mind was screaming at me to take advantage of this interview because this may be our only chance. I tried to tell Chief to take my line of questioning but he was anxious and intent on his own direction.

You have to understand this situation. The Lao had no idea this witness was going to say he was a guard for POWs during the war. If they had been forewarned, there was no way we would have had this access to him. He would have been pre-screened and told what he could reveal. This was a unique situation that had presented itself out of nowhere.

Chief continued his line of questioning and gained multiple descriptions of POWs the old man had allegedly guarded. An hour later the Lao officials told us we needed to take a break. During this time, the witness was taken off to the side and spoken to. When he returned, he could not remember details such as years or descriptions. He claimed his memory had become fuzzy and was failing him. The officials then stopped the interview "because the witness was tired."

Our worst imagined scenario had become a reality. For the next three years we tried to locate and re-interview that witness. For three years Lao officials made excuses as to why the witness was not available—implausible excuses. A typical attempt to find the witness would consist of us landing at the village, a Lao official telling us to wait by the aircraft, as the official departing into the village. After a half hour, the official would come back and tell us that the witness had a pig die, was sick, was traveling, needed an appendectomy and went to Vientiane, or was now senile. These were all actual explanations given with straight faces and in serious tones. There was no consistency in the excuse which generated no confidence in the story.

We never had the opportunity again to interview that witness and I always felt it was an opportunity lost. Over the next few years Chief and I discussed that interview often and the possibility of having done it differently. If that witness had provided credible information in our first interview, it had the potential to lead to the recovery of multiple POWs.

* * *

Operations in Laos brought many unforeseen planning considerations. Seasonal limitations, team composition, and aircraft usage all had to be factored into our plans. Efficiency maximized our time and minimized our operating expenses.

The seasonal and environmental limitations of operations in Southeast Asian were significant. For my team to work efficiently during the monsoon (wet) season required limited flight times and cases at elevations below the cloud base. Also a number of cases required only ground transportation. Then, if required, we could continue to investigate even under a low cloud base. Our target regions had to be alternated to coincide with the seasonal weather patterns. Savannakhet Province was located on the central plain and conducive to wet weather operations. Almost all other provinces required operations at higher elevations. These investigations would be hindered by the buildup of clouds on the mountains, which limited movement by air.

Investigations during the dry season coincided with the rice growing season. During this period farmers moved to live near their rice fields. This required additional time to locate the village chief and witnesses requested. This coordination took time away from the current day's investigations and hampered the flexible flow of the IE from village to village.

The optimum and most productive period for our investigations was just after the rice harvest was complete. Most laborers were back in their villages and we enjoyed a flexible and fluid investigation schedule

*   *   *

The physical stamina of the team augmenters also became a serious issue. The IE frequently conducted foot movements over extremely demanding mountainous and jungle terrain—always in a hot and humid environment. On multiple occasions, augmenters could not complete the foot movements and had to be sent back to the aircraft with Lao guides. The remainder of the team always continued the mission. It became essential to screen augmenters upon arrival at JTF-FA to assess their general fitness and mental toughness. Then the strongest Special Forces Medic and Marine Explosive Ordnance Disposal expert would be assigned to the IE. This provided the best potential for completing our mission.

Use of the Lao MI-17 did not *generally* hamper IE operations. During the wet season it was a hindrance due to the lack of adequate landing zones to support the larger helicopter. The MI-17 carried a lot of weight on its back axle and would easily sink into wet ground. Also, the strong rotor wash, generated by it main rotor, required a landing zone away from fields or buildings. Often, we had to pay a villager for damage to his roof or rice field.

The MI-17 was an "animal" of a machine that seemed to prove that anything could fly if you put a big enough engine on it. It was built rugged with one big rotor above the main cabin and one tail rotor on a long boom. Due to its durability it was used for transporting troops and equipment. Passengers could see and feel the aircraft shake and vibrate wildly as the engine built speed. With another burst of rotor speed, the aircraft would lurch from the ground and hover as if it were trying to balance itself. Slowly, the nose would lower and the vibrating hulk would begin to move forward. Fuel or other fluids would drip from the ceiling from tubing we couldn't see. The fumes from the fuel filled the interior of the cabin and you had no confidence of ever reaching the ground safely.

A typical landing zone for the MI-17 helicopter -- a workhorse but scary in comparison to American aircraft.

The Recovery Elements routinely used the MI-17 to ferry their personnel and equipment, but understandably had little faith in the safety of the aircraft. Periodically, the Lao aircrews gave safety and orientation briefings to everyone in the base camp in an attempt to generate confidence. I was always annoyed when the IE got caught up in the event. My team wasn't overly concerned with the MI-17. After all, we were already hanging off the skids of the "Squirrel" to reach areas of jungle and mountains. These were pretty extreme operations. The MI-17 was our ride home and the safe end of a dangerous day. To help with general confidence, myself and Yan Collins would attempt to ride in the MI-17 more often than normal.

The MI-17 actually proved itself to be extremely durable. On one occasion, it had landed in a pasture near a village we were visiting. As we waited to conduct an interview, the aircrew decided to pivot the aircraft to facilitate leaving. Suddenly, there was a loud blast which reminded me of a huge weed trimmer. The MI-17 had pivoted and run its tail rotor right through a bushy fruit tree. Small pieces of chopped leaves and branches showered down across the pasture. As the helicopter pulled away, there was a perfect crescent shape left in the tree. Yet, the helicopter flew home that night with no problem.

Our MI-17 Crew; notice the black soot behind the engines.

The most terrifying aspect of flying in the MI-17 was when the Lao pilots would try to get out of a mountainous area during inclement weather. It was not unusual for us to arrive in a valley during a break in the weather and later get socked in by overcast clouds and heavy rain. The MI-17's answer to this problem was to put everyone on board and rise straight up until they got above the clouds. Then, the pilot would transport us to the next location. Two *small* problems existed with this plan. First, you ran the risk of hitting something on the way up because you couldn't see any obstructions. Second, if you had a mechanical emergency and needed to land there would be no safe way to descend through the clouds to find a clear landing area.

The cargo space in the back of the MI-17 was loaded with team equipment and convenience items like lawn chairs and coolers to endure each day. These comfort items would be used by the crew as they whiled away long hours at the aircraft. Meanwhile, the Investigation Element trekked through the jungles or interviewed in villages.

The Lao were constantly "grocery" shopping and the cargo on the return trip could include pigs, goats, chickens, ducks, half developed eggs, snakes, big lizards, and once even a cow. There was no refrigeration where we were operating, so the meat went straight from the knife to the cooking pot.

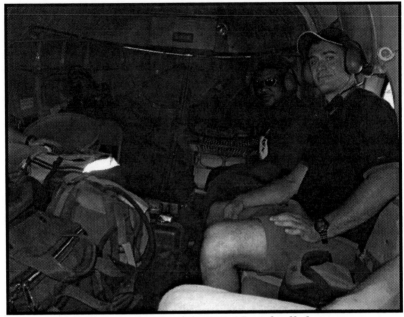

Riding in the back of the MI-17 with all the gear.

Occasionally, on our trips to Khammouan Province, a provincial official would accompany us during our investigations. He was about five feet five inches tall, always wore green camouflage, and was very stocky. He was obviously very fit and had a pronounced round jaw. We nicknamed him the "Beast Master" because he was the ultimate food scrounger. He couldn't help himself. If he saw a hole in the ground, he would just shove his hand and arm down there to root around and see if he could pull something out. Usually it was fresh water crabs, toads or snakes. At other times, he would take his AK-47 and go squirrel or bird hunting. He would regularly fill the back of the MI-17 with plants and animals. It was interesting to come back to the aircraft and see his latest acquisition.

On one occasion, Becky became extremely upset because there were two lambs in a cargo pod on the side of the MI-17 kicking and bleating. She refused to get into the aircraft unless they let the lambs go. She even offered to pay for them so she could release them on the spot. The officials finally chose not to purchase the lambs and avert an issue. Another occasion there was a big burlap sack moving on the floor and I asked to see inside. It was a massive python of some sort. He was destined for the stewpot.

Goats tied-up and ready to be loaded on the MI-17.

In 2002, Sammy, Greg Parmele, and I flew down to a village along the Cambodian border. We were in Attapu Province, Laos, to interview some witnesses for a crash site on the Cambodian side of the border. The Lao villagers regularly crossed the border to hunt and fish but border crossing was considered illegal. The officials said this was a dangerous area; therefore, they would transport the witnesses about five miles from the border to a village where we would wait for them. During our wait we sat down for a Pepsi at a small soup diner. Sammy told me to follow him to the back room. As I looked in the dark space, I could hear things moving but couldn't see them. As my eyes adjusted I saw three big Iguana type lizards with twine tethers tied around their necks. Sammy explained it was big business to find these in the jungle and sell them for $200 each. They were considered a delicacy and like the python—destined for the stewpot!

When the MI-17 arrived with the witnesses, it landed in a small clearing behind the diner. As we approached, the Lao officials explained we would do the interview inside the aircraft. Inside four fearful middle aged men sat on a bench seat on the left side of the aircraft. I entered with Greg and Sammy and sat on the other side. A provincial official with an exposed handgun sat on the left end of their bench and scowled at them with every question. It was like interviewing SGT Schulz from "Hogan's Heroes." They looked at us and said they "knew nothing!" They claimed they never crossed the border because it would be illegal and didn't know of a crash site. We knew they were under duress and not being truthful.

* * *

From January to February of 2001, I had the opportunity to accompany a Vietnam Investigation Element to Hanoi where we would conduct a series of investigations. Over a ten-day period we would work from Hanoi southward toward Danang. Danang was the location of China Beach during the war and I looked forward to seeing what was there.

We arrived in Hanoi and the social environment was much different than that in Laos. You could tell the Vietnamese had received a dose of commercialism from the Americans during the war. Everywhere I saw hustle and bustle and hard working people. Streets were packed with crowds of people on bicycles, scooters, and motorcycles moving through the city.

We moved south, via road, in two vans which left me white knuckled as I clung to the door handle and seat. We sped down the road barely avoiding a head on collision every time we approached any oncoming traffic. The days were spent on the road and the evenings in nice hotels. The food and rooms were good and I felt spoiled.

One morning we were leaving the hotel to conduct some business and passed through the kitchen area. On the floor was a pile of thirty-one (counted them) dead and wiggling rats—rats for cooking. I did not eat any food dishes that I could not identify after that discovery.

We attempted to investigate a number of cases. All interviews were conducted in our hotels and after officials arrived with the required witnesses. It was a very sterile interview technique and there was no ability to freelance. The investigations prior to my departure were all fruitless, but I had learned much about the limitations imposed by the Vietnamese on the Investigation Teams.

We did spend one day in a fishing boat on the Gulf of Tonkin. We had interviewed some locals on a beach who described an area fishermen had to avoid with their nets. They claimed it was common knowledge that an airplane was on the ocean floor there. We then accompanied the fisherman to the area and dragged a big grappling hook across the ocean floor. We snagged something solid and took a GPS reading to identify the spot. Later a dive team would come to inspect the area.

The ten days went quickly and I had to fly back to Oahu. I would have only ten days to prepare for our next JFA to Laos. The Detachment Two Commander, LTC Rennie Quarry, stopped with his chartered MI-17 to pick me up and we flew on to Danang.

We stayed at the Furama Resort, a Five-Star Resort on China Beach. The hotel was beautiful. It had heavy marble floors and walls accented by shutters and blinds made of dark red woods. The hotel was centered on a lighted pool and fountain with palm trees draped over the edges.

It was beautiful by any standard and had an exotic oriental feel. I sat down that night with LTC Quarry, Chief Pedro Gonzales, and Tech. Sgt. Robert Flynn, from the Detachment 2 under a cabaña near the beach. We ate a great dinner of seafood, fish, and drank some good beer. The conversation centered on home and what we enjoyed or looked forward to doing. We said our goodbyes and the next day I was off to Oahu via commercial flight. The DET 2 team was off to Hanoi.

*　　*　　*

One of the first unique cases we recommended for excavation involved the crew of an F-4 Phantom that had been flying over Savannakhet Province. They had ejected after being hit by ground fire. Both crewmembers made it to the ground under their canopies and landed in the trees. The aircraft then crashed into the mountain much higher up.

Once on the ground, both pilots made contact with an Air America helicopter that attempted to pick them up. One pilot ran to a clearing, boarded the helicopter, and was rescued. A search and rescue helicopter located the second pilot on a spur of the mountain under 100-foot trees. They dropped a jungle penetrater through the jungle canopy, got the pilot on the hoist, and began to winch him up.

The Load Master controlling the winch recalled that when the pilot cleared the trees he could see he was only hanging onto the rescue harness by his hands. They continued to pull him up but when he was about thirty feet short of the aircraft, he lost his grip, and fell back into the treetops. Nothing more was heard from this pilot and it was assumed he must have fallen three-hundred feet to the ground. Enemy troops had reached the area and no attempt was made for a ground search to recover the body. He was presumed to have died from the fall. This crewman was considered Last Known Alive, because he was last seen alive.

Previous teams had investigated this case by visiting the crash site, locating an aircraft canopy in a village along the road, and observing an old revolver supposedly from the crew. We continued the investigation by revisiting the villages and re-interviewing the old witnesses. We also located one of the ejection seats in another abandoned village along the road.

Through our investigation we confirmed that both pilots had landed on separate spurs (small ridges) of the mountain. One crewman ran to a clearing and was rescued. The other was on a spur the locals referred to as "the place where the American died." We needed to visit that site to search for any evidence to prove or disprove the pilot had actually died there.

It was mid-afternoon when we gathered the team from the two different helicopters and looked up at the hill we would have to scale in a timely fashion. The jungle was thick on both sides of the ridge and the hilltop itself was clear of mature trees due to periodic dry rice farming. The field had last been used two years prior. In the interim, thick grass and small trees had sprung up in a dense maze.

We conducted a quick check to ensure we had a compass, radios, water, camera, fifty-foot measuring tape, and Global Positioning System (GPS). Then we began to head up a streambed on the left side of the ridge. The plan was to avoid the thickest jungle as long as possible. It was the dry season so the bedrock stream bottom was relatively easy to climb. We pushed upward in a single file and the heat began to affect some of the weaker team members.

Becky was our Army analyst, always motivated, but had difficulty with the climbs and in the heat of the jungle. Becky moved toward the rear of the file and Gunny Carabello assisted her climb. In an instant she slipped and fell and her face crashed into the rocks. When she rose, blood oozed from her now black and blue face. With an irritated curse she pushed past the obvious pain and continued on her way toward the top. Drenched in sweat but pushing hard, we reached a point adjacent to the field. We then turned right and crawled on our hands and knees straight up a near vertical slope for about fifty meters to the crest.

While a Lao witness oriented me and Sammy to the area, the remainder of the team took a break under the canopy of small trees and cane. We pushed our way through the pig trails as the witness explained that there used to be a clump of sticks where local folklore said the American was. He said no one had ever actually seen an American pilot, but that was the story. He also said that during the clearing and planting of the dry rice field he had found a boot sole. Next, we were also shown the stump of a very large tree that the American had supposedly been hung up in after he parachuted to the ground. An old man showed us a strap he had taken from the gear that had been in the tree.

The team then did a random search of the vicinity and found nothing. We then did organized line searches and still found nothing. Next, we relied upon the location of the tree stump and referred to the narrative of the Search and Rescue (SAR) attempt. They estimated that once they had the pilot on the hoist they had drifted around fifty meters. We speculated the pilot would want to be picked up from the top of the spur which was about twenty meters from the stump. Don, the Squirrel pilot, and I discussed seasonal winds, lines of drift, and a desire to drift away from the road located approximately five-hundred meters to the north. Based on this sheer raw common sense analysis, we recommended a location about fifty meters uphill from the tree for excavation. This was the last shot we had to resolve this case.

A few JFAs later, this case was on the excavation list because it had priority as a Last Known Alive Case. The probability of success was very low. If the Excavation Team could finish their primary case early, they would go to this site and use the remainder of their time. The anthropologist and Team Leader came to see me in Pattaya on the way into Laos. They asked me why I had recommended it for excavation. I drew out the case on a napkin and made a fist using the back of

Lao jungle; dark, damp, and alive with the sound of critters.

my hand as the example. The knuckles of the clenched fist were the top of the mountain and each finger was a spur. At the bottom of the fingers was the road. I showed where both parachutes had landed in the trees and where villagers had found pieces of a pilot's life support items on the hill. I explained this was our best shot—our only shot. It wasn't much, but this was our best and last chance to deliver for this family.

The Recovery Element finished their primary site early. When they went to this site on the spur, their expectations were small. Sammy was the linguist for this dig team and he told us the story afterwards. During the initial setup of the site an area is always designated for a latrine and break area. A sweep with a metal detector was done to look for mines and other Unexploded Ordnance. During the sweep of the latrine area, they got a hit and immediately dug up the pilot's wedding ring with a personal inscription from his wife. They continued to dig and found little else but watch parts and other small items. No remains of any sort were found. Since the site was located on the side of a spur it was speculated that years of rain and erosion could have washed the remains down hill. Also, the remote location would have provided ample opportunity for scavenging and dispersing by wild animals and domestic pigs. Lastly, acidic soil had the ability to degrade remains over time.

The wedding ring was returned to the crewman's wife in the states. I was told she was extremely grateful for our efforts. It was the best we could do for the family. I was happy we had sent something home.

*   *   *

We had been on a long day of interviews in Phin District, Savannakhet Province, in search of another F-4 Phantom. This aircraft has been missing since 1971 after it departed Korat Airbase in Thailand and never returned home. It was in a flight of two aircraft with a mission to conduct bombing runs over Savannakhet Province, Laos. Prior to its second run on a target the F-4 was seen to explode. There were no parachutes observed or beeper detected from the two man crew.

Smoke filled skies from burning fields.

Bill Forsythe believed the crash site had been located much further to the north, only to have that correlation later proven to be incorrect. Now the investigation had become a game of cat and mouse to find the correct village, at the right time, and to have the right witness be on hand. We needed that unknown witness to give us the correct information to find the crash site. What we did know was the site was somewhere within the expanse of a wide open valley floor with a large mountain looming above. The mountain resembled a huge plateau with vertical sides and a flatter summit.

Our investigation was conducted during the dry season and rice fields were being cleared for the upcoming planting season. The days were extremely hot and smoke from farmers burning the chaff from their fields filled the entire sky with a haze. Thick plumes of smoke forced our helicopter to steer around to maintain visibility. On the ground were huge brush fires with bright flames jumping skyward. The sun was a hot pink color as it shined through the smoke.

In our third village of the day, we sat in a circle under the shade produced by the MI-17 tail boom. There, a few village elders told us the story of an airplane that had crashed on the edge of the village. The plane remained intact and the pilot was still alive but injured. The villagers then rushed the airplane and cut off his head. The pilot was buried nearby and the elders believed they could still locate the gravesite. The description of this event did not correlate to any losses of which we were aware. From our study of the data bases we would later determine this to be a French or Thai pilot and not American.

The Thai's had established a small Air Corps flying T-38 aircraft. Occasionally, we would come across their crash sites during our other investigations. It was extremely interesting to find these sites and more than once we had heard of a man falling from the sky near one of these crashes. They did not have ejection seats and the injured pilot would bail out of the plane and apparently not successfully deploy his parachute.

Late that afternoon, we sent the MI-17 back to the base camp. We had decided to use the Squirrel to stop at one last village with Sammy, Pierce, myself, and a Lao official. We flew a few miles and then landed outside a progressive and bustling village. This village was located on a road and surrounded by tillable land and therefore had prospered beyond the norm. They had maintained the normal building style of huts on stilts, but some roofs were tin. Their improved, wood-plank floors did not creak and strain under the weight of one person.

We sat on a few stumps under a shade tree, in the middle of the village, and met with three male elders. They were dressed in their evening attire of a Sarong, cheap flip-flops, and loose-collared shirts. One old man puffed on a crude pipe and seemed very content with himself. We were short on time and Sammy jumped the normal interview protocol and got straight to the point. His first question was if there were any crash sites in the village area.

Immediately they nodded excitedly and told the story of an airplane that had crashed outside of their village. It had happened in the middle of the night and the huge resulting explosion rocked the village. The next day the villagers went to the area of the explosion and found a huge crater. Dogs were scavenging the area and running around with pieces of remains from the people in the airplane. They vividly described a dog with a piece of skull and dental remains in a ditch near the site.

We asked if they had anything from the aircraft and an old villager excitedly ran off to his hut. Shortly he returned with a survival hatchet he had gotten from the crash. I had never seen one of these and it was the bit of proof that we had more than just a crash site. Unfortunately, we had run out of time for the day. Dusk was approaching, and we had to get back to camp before dark. Therefore, we made an appointment to visit the site the next day.

Village center: Always happy Lao pigs.

Early the next day we arrived with the entire team and landed to the north of the village about five-hundred meters. Fifty meters from the aircraft, across a dried rice paddy, was a large crater, about twenty meters across. We walked to the edge of the crater and inside we saw a heavily crusted clay and mud-baked circle. In the very middle was one strut from an airplane sticking straight up. The villagers said that was the only piece of wreckage they couldn't get out to sell to the local metals buyers. Reggie immediately focused on that strut and said, "You know, if we get that strut out, there will be a serial number on the bottom housing that will prove at least our aircraft type." Half the team began to assemble the shovels and picks to pry that strut loose. Pierce and I began to search the edge of the crater.

As Pierce and I searched, we soon found pieces of flight suit zipper and cloth. Then in the woodline, about ten meters from the crater, we found boot heels from American boots. This was evidence there was definitely an aircrew in this aircraft. The date, time, and description of the event were also consistent with the description of our case. This was likely our aircraft.

Pierce and I returned to the strut where the remainder team members were laboring to gain some headway. "Reggie, we probably don't need that strut with the other things we know," I said.

Reggie defiantly exclaimed, "Oh, HELLLL NO! We're getting this thing out!" They had been busting their butts under the unforgiving heat of a clear Lao day and were not prepared to give up the effort. Pierce and I jumped in to give the others a rest. The clay in the pit clung to the pick, shovel, and the strut and progress came a half-inch at a time.

I would have given anything to have a tractor and a log chain right then to rip this thing from the ground. In its place, we had eight team members drenched in sweat, covered in wet and drying clay, with chests heaving from the strain. We sought to catch our breath and rotated two men at a time into the hole. Finally, that strut began to move back and forth but the ground was not ready to give it up. Late in the afternoon with pry bars made from stout branches and the pick and shovels, we heaved as a group and removed it from its clay prison. A half-hour later we had a few definitive numbers taken from the heavily corroded metal.

This was a big find and after an excavation it would likely result in an aircrew going home to their families. That strut had become a symbol for the team overcoming an obstacle together.

Reggie digging for the strut; Pierce (left) and Doc (right).

For the next two years we would talk about the strut and the challenge of removing it from the ground each time another obstacle presented itself. Someone would always say, "This is nothing. Remember that F-4 strut we dug out of that pit?"

*   *   *

This F-4 site was excavated on the next JFA but operations suspended due to the heavy amount of clay in the soil. The clay was so hard it could not be screened. To make any progress at all required an abundant water source from which to pump water into the screens. It was determined that an excavation during the wet season may be more feasible. The next wet season the excavation teams had set up screening stations and the clay clogged the screens. The DET3 Commander informed me months later that an RE had again tried to excavate the site during the dry season. The DET 3 Commander was frustrated and not sure when the excavation could be completed.

Much later I learned that the excavation had been extremely challenging and had produced only small bone fragments. This was extremely disheartening since the evidence at the site definitely indicated the crew was in the aircraft at the time of impact. Recovery of enough remains to make a final DNA match was a necessity. A determination would have to be made on how to proceed.

*   *   *

During this JFA, we were scheduled to investigate the loss of a UH-1H Huey helicopter. Other teams had searched for this site for the past two years. This site involved the attempted insertion of half of a Special Forces Prairie Fire team. Prairie Fire teams were reconnaissance teams comprised of South Vietnamese troops with U.S. Special Forces advisors. These teams were sent covertly up to twenty miles into Laos to report on NVA movements along the Ho Chi Minh trail. On this occasion, two helicopter gunships attempted to lay fire on the intended landing zone but received heavy fire from the ground. The two Hueys had followed behind the gunships and quickly banked to exit the area. The first did a sharp turn and was successful. The second did a slow turn, was hit, went into a nose dive and then crashed and exploded. No search and rescue effort reached the site due to heavy enemy activity in the area.

After multiple investigations and interviews no evidence had been located to suggest the site was located at or near its record location. Therefore, by a process of elimination of known sites, it had been determined that a site 10 kilometers to the northwest must be the correct one. That site was scheduled for excavation on the next JFA.

I had asked to reinvestigate the recorded loss location after a talk with the Detachment 3 Commander. He expressed concerns they would excavate a site with little or no evidence. I discussed the issue with Bill Forsythe, and we agreed to try one last investigation near the record loss location. After all, the record loss location came from a Special Forces soldier on the surviving bird. It seemed unlikely they could be ten kilometers off on their estimation of the crash site, especially since both Hueys were near their planned landing zone.

This suspected loss area was a large slab of lava rock that ran for three to four-thousand meters north and south between the border of Savannakhet and Salavan Provinces, Laos. We had investigated often in this area while looking for multiple sites. Near the peak of this flow was elephant grass and tall trees making navigation extremely difficult. To make matters worse, it had been heavily bombed during the war and there were numerous metal hulks of destroyed vehicles.

We had interviewed at two nearby villages with no success. Then we set out to walk the trails and flows in a ground search to see if we could locate wreckage. We were looking for any evidence to indicate a helicopter crash site was in the area. As we worked through thickets and ravines, we saw leftover evidence of a military depot in the area. Communication wires, old radios, 50-gallon drums, and considerable unexploded mortar rounds. This evidence was consistent with the record loss narrative of a heavy NVA presence in the area. Although we found intriguing residue from the war, we still lacked any evidence of our lost Huey.

We then stopped at a small clearing to formulate a new search plan. We crouched in a circle and conferred with the Lao officials. I looked up to see a young Lao man and his little boy standing next to us. They must have emerged from the tall grass along the trail and moseyed over to see what was going on. They were dressed in shorts, torn T-shirts, rubber thong sandals and each carried a typical machete to cut trails.

I asked the Lao official to ask him if he knew of any crash sites in the area around us. That was where the luck of the moment shone through again. If that official had thought this guy knew anything, he would never have asked the question. If the guy had said, "Yes, there are," in some nondescript way, the official likely would have told us, "Nope, but we can ask at the next village." In this case, the guy hesitated and then excitedly pointed at the small ridgeline to our front. He shook his head up an down in affirmation and had a big smile on his face.

Where there was one BLU-26 there were sure to be more.

The young villager said the land belonged to the village chief and they had just started clearing it the previous year. That was when they had found helicopter wreckage. We obtained the chief's name, and a District official walked to the village and made an appointment for him to show us the site.

Meanwhile, the young man walked us over another knoll, about four-hundred meters, to a freshly cut field in the forest. The newly felled trees were piled in all directions and created an impenetrable abbatti. To make matters worse, there was unexploded ordnance everywhere. Mortar rounds and cluster munitions had been stacked in piles by the locals as they cleared the field. We then decided it would be prudent to wait for the next day. It would be safer and save time to have the chief guide us to the site.

Becky Sorrell, Adam Pierce, and Pat Clifford analyzing their cases late into the night at the Boulapha Base Camp.

What we found the next day was the *Holy Grail* for an investigation team. A site with extensive evidence that many had searched for but all had failed to find. The crash site contained a large amount of helicopter wreckage and life support items. On our hands and knees we scratched through the foliage, and just under the surface of the wet ground, we found the TA-50 (personal tactical equipment) that the Prairie Fire team had worn, including Load Carrying Equipment (LCE), helmet parts, boot soles, loaded M-16 magazines, and on and on. Finally, we found a date plate from a dashboard component which positively correlated the crash site to a UH-

1H Huey. The aircraft type and location correlated to our missing aircraft.

This was a good day, and yet, a very sad day. As a Ranger, I could just imagine their last moments as I knew exactly how they felt during their air assault mission—nervous anticipation, excitement, and determination. Their mission ended in tragedy. These soldiers and crewmembers would be going home after a successful excavation on the next JFA.

Vietnamese/Lao Trilateral delegation.

There was a report that one of the crewmen was actually alive after the crash and buried by North Vietnamese soldier by a large tree located near the crash site. Detachment Two in

Vietnam brought a group of veterans over to meet us in Laos and hopefully point out the site of the burial.

We met them at the border with the MI-17 and flew to the crash site located thirty minutes by air to the south. There we waited as the veterans walked the area and then decided upon a large tree where the pilot was allegedly buried.

We then spent the remainder of the day digging a shallow trench in the designated location but did not find any evidence to suggest a crewmember was buried at the site. This was another frustrating end to the investigation to that point. We had found the main crash site but there was another loose end to which we had no immediate solution. It would take many more months of interviews and investigation to bring closure to this case.

*   *   *

In April of 2001, I was in Savannakhet, Laos, for report writing. We had completed our report writing requirements at midnight prior to our much anticipated return to Hawaii. No sooner had I entered my room to get some sleep then there was a knock on the door. When I opened it, the Deputy Commander for Detachment 3, Al Teel, was standing there with a concerned look on his face. He then informed me that there had been a helicopter crash in Vietnam—the Detachment 2 staff had been killed.

The next day I boarded a C-130 that was granted an exception to departure procedure by the Lao and flew to the DET 1 Headquarters in Hanoi. There I performed duties as the operations officer to provide continuity to the very confused and emotional situation resulting from the death of seven Americans. Also lost were nine Vietnamese colleagues from the Vietnamese Office for Seeking Missing Persons (VNOSMP). The phones rang off the hook continuously with people expressing their concern, reporters trying to get a story, or mortuary businesses try to get in on the action. It was a madhouse hindered by the fact that none of us spoke Vietnamese. We had to push all of those calls to two Detachment linguists to handle.

I also had to organize the memorial service and portions of the Repatriation ceremony with the American Embassy-Hanoi. It was my first opportunity to see the inner circle of an embassy and it was gratifying to see the quality of people who sat at the table of the Embassy Team Meeting. They worked hard to ensure the memorial service was befitting of the Americans and Vietnamese who were lost.

Vietnamese chartered MI-17 used by Detachment 2 in Hanoi.

The most challenging issue was the identification of the bodies. This was complicated by the fact the victims' personal belongings had separated from the bodies. This happened somewhere between the crash site and the morgue in Hanoi. Upon arrival, all the bodies were naked. None had any jewelry or clothing with them. This made identification of the remains very difficult for the anthropologist (Dave Rankin). He was trying his damnedest to correctly separate the Americans from the Vietnamese and correctly identify each individual. In the Buddhist religion, the family just wanted a body to bury and was not particularly worried about which one. Upon death, they considered the body no more than a husk and needed to bury the remains by the third day. The Americans, of course, wanted positive identification to return the correct remains to the appropriate family. A serious problem would result if a mistake was made during a preliminary identification and a Buddhist family buried an American body. The Buddhist customs had to be balanced with the wait for dental records to arrive from the U.S. The dental record s would provide the evidence with which to make a definitive identification. As a result of Dave Rankin's' exhaustive work, no mistakes were made.

The memorial ceremony in Hanoi was well attended by both Americans and Vietnamese officials. After the ceremony was completed, we loaded the flag-covered coffins on the aircraft for the flight back home. It was a tear-filled departure for the guys that had worked in Hanoi. Personally, I was tired. These were the same buddies I had eaten dinner with at the Furama Hotel in Danang. We had talked of careers and families—now they were gone.

On our way back to Hawaii, we stopped in Guam at around 2 a.m. A flag waving patriotic crowd was waiting on the tarmac of the airstrip to greet us. LTC Childress, our Public Affairs Officer, addressed the crowd, the airplane refueled, and we continued on our way back to Hawaii.

*   *   *

Chapter 4
Into the Darkness

The core members of the Laos Investigation Element had changed over a short period of months in 2001. A new and cohesive group including Suriyan Collins, Greg Parmele, Adam Pierce, and Sammy Vilaysane, had developed over a series of JFAs. They were physically very strong and brought an intensity that took us to a new level. This group would provide the endurance, fearlessness, and competitive spirit, to reach the remote sites. They were also blessed with individual talents that empowered our investigation plans.

Master Sergeant Suriyan Collins was an Army Non-Commissioned Officer in his mid-thirties and of Thai decent. He stood about five foot ten inches tall and was a totally focused and professional Assistant Team Leader. He was also fluent in Lao and Thai which made him absolutely invaluable to the team. His combat arms experience made the difference in planning, safety, and equipment preparation. Never did you have to question his focus or will to succeed.

Sergeant First Class Greg Parmele was also an Army Non-Commissioned Officer in his mid-thirties. He was fluent in Thai and functional in Lao and Cambodian. He stood about six foot one and spent much of his spare time running, hiking and biking the island of Oahu. He was a great analyst and interviewer. He also had a knack for making the officials and witnesses relax enough to trust our intentions.

Sergeant Adam Pierce was an Army NCO in his early twenties. He was functional in the Lao language; about five foot eleven, lean and muscular. He was a team analyst, smart, ambitious and gung-ho. He was ready for any challenge and I relied on him to come with me on the tough climbs.

Staff Sergeant Sengchanh (Sammy) Vilaysane was an Army NCO and the cog of the team. He was of Lao descent and our linguist for almost all interviews and negotiations. He was trusted by the Lao and easily endeared himself to the village elders where ever we went. He was shorter at around five foot six and heavy around the middle. We called him "Fat Sammy." Sammy was scared of heights and no adventurer, but he brought success to the team that was both immeasurable and invaluable.

Later, we added SGT Rudy Alvarez, a young Marine NCO and Intelligence Analyst. He stood around six feet tall and a solid two-hundred pounds. He was a funny guy who was always seeking competition at the ping pong table or while trekking up a mountain. He was a strong and capable addition to the team.

If I had to describe myself during this period, it would be focused, tireless, pensive, experienced, and competent. The Lao described me as "strong like bull." This was the result of a two day climb up a mountain to a remote crash site in Khammouan Province. Even with a rucksack of equipment, I out climbed a set of young Lao guides carrying nothing but a machete.

Every evening the team would huddle to discuss the successes of the previous day and the game plan for the next. We could not underestimate the basic nuts and bolts of moving men and machines over long distances and onto remote landing sites throughout Laos. We factored in the relationship and daily attitude of national, province, district, and local officials and the will and ability of the MI-17 aircrew to complete their mission. Previously, we had two incidents where the Lao pilot refused to fly us where we needed to go. On the first occasion, the pilot lost his nerve. On the second occasion, the pilot claimed to not have the skills to land on a mountain. Within a few days, the pilots were replaced and the missions completed. Other variables were the tribal makeup of Laos. This mix included the somewhat hospitable Hmong and the uncooperative and distrusting Lao Teung tribes. The Lao Teung culturally did not like outsiders. I wrote home often with stories of our challenges.

Mon, 26 Mar 2001
Good morning from Laos,
   It's a rainy morning and I ran over, got a cup of coffee (O.K. two) and got to the commo building to send a msg before the day gets away from me. Looks like the rain is trying to hamper us today but we have a lot of work to do regardless within driving distance.
   Wow, it is really pouring rain now - thunder and lightning also. We had an interesting morning yesterday. We flew to a Lao Teung village in central Laos where the Lao don't like outsiders. Not just foreigners but even other Lao. Apparently for generations there was tribal discrimination. We landed and a crowd ran to both helos (one is a big Lao army transport) and asked what the hell we were doing there. Our officials all dressed in their Laos Army uniforms tried to explain (we had national, province, and district officials) and the area village chief had his guys watching with AK-47's. He said not only were we not supposed to be there but we could not leave until we got clearance from the main area chief. So, we got detained under guard for half a day until the area chief, in a village three miles away, decided we could leave.

Many hours were spent pouring over maps, photos historical references under a dull light bulb swirling with moths, termites and mosquitoes. We were never satisfied to enter an area after just one planning session. We made sure we were familiar with all cases in a geographic area. This meant each and every day could have an immediate twist which could send us in an unexpected direction.

(Left to right) Adam Pierce, Greg Paremele, Rex Hodges, myself, and Yan Collins. Receiving analysis from Hawaii via a satellite link regarding evidence we located in Laos.

These quick shifts in direction made the Lao officials very uncomfortable. Yan and Sammy were very adept at reassuring the officials of our intent to pursue an undefined lead which had just presented itself. To their credit, for the most part, the officials supported our fluid style of operation without knowing what it could generate. Surprises were hard to manage.

This style of investigation also was not readily accepted in the Operations Directorate at JTF-FA. Joe Patterson was the

Assistant Operations Director and had been the Cambodian Team Leader throughout the late 1990's. During that period, you were to move fast and pursue written and defined leads on many specific cases. That showed attention to many cases and briefed well to the public. We had broken that restrictive mold and were supported by Bill Forsythe, in the Lao analysis department and Lieutenant Colonel George, the new Operations Director. This fluid style took us to villages, located witnesses, and brought finality to cases as the opportunity presented itself. This wasn't a political or strategic style—it was operational, tactical, and dictated by the men in the field.

Pushing the envelope of safety.

Reaching the remote sites took mutual trust between pilots and team, and we rehearsed and discussed our techniques often. In the work my team did, the helicopter rarely put two skids on the ground for any operation—it was likely one or no skids.

Going in we had to jump and then have the chain saws lowered in by chain or rope. This allowed you to cut trees to allow the helicopter to get close enough to the ground to climb back up, usually off of a stump or rock. This was very dangerous and there was no medical search and rescue team anywhere in Laos that would come to our aid. If someone was injured, we would have to carry him out to a clearing. That was complicated because the mountains did not have clearings. That was the problem we wrestled with—how to conduct dangerous operations with no good plan for a medical evacuation.

Stepping on the skid – a hovering LZ.

That was also why we always had a Special Forces Medic with us. They were masters at stabilizing a patient and keeping him alive until he could reach a higher standard of care. To qualify as a Special Forces Medic, a man had to keep a goat alive after it had been administered a small caliber gunshot wound. Not any gunshot wound—the skin would be pulled and stretched to the side, a gunshot administered, and the skin released back into position. Therefore, the gunshot was not where the hole in the skin was located.

Unexploded ordnance was always a threat.

We often discussed amongst ourselves and the pilots what we would do in a life threatening situation. Of particular concern were the most critical injuries, such as a severed limb. There were only two answers to the problem. The first option was to attempt to reach the main base camp. It could be hours away but there was a U.S. trauma doctor on duty there. The second option was to crash the border into Thailand to a better medical facility. This was the ultimate extreme since the pilots assumed they would never be allowed back into Laos, but to save a life they would do it.

*   *   *

The ground raced by on both sides of our small helicopter as we raced down the Xekong River gorge, in south central Laos. We were heading east in an attempt to get back to our base camp. We had been about forty miles to the west to a series of small mountains along the Vietnam border. There we were searching for an Army Green Beret lost in a helicopter crash and missing since the Vietnam War. For a week we had waited in our base camp in Salavan City for a break in the weather. Dark low clouds had settled from a typhoon in the South China Sea. Earlier in the morning the rain stopped and the clouds lifted to reveal the mountains, which separated us from the remote area along the Vietnam/Laos border. After consultation with the helicopter pilots, we decided to make a run to the east. We skimmed the treetops just under a heavy cloud ceiling and dropped into the river gorge. Once in the gorge, we scooted up the river valley under the cover of a dark cottony blanket of clouds which obscured the tops of the mountains.

Now it was late afternoon and Eric, our New Zealand pilot, had told my small team to get on board because the clouds were looking darker to the west—we needed to go. Sammy my linguist, Pierce my analyst, and two Lao officials were in the back seat. I occupied the copilot seat on the left. We took off and zoomed down the river valley. The clouds had settled in and now there was the sensation of flying down a tube—steep slopes on both sides, rushing water underneath, and a ceiling of thick heavy clouds right above our heads. We hoped to get to a bend in the river where it abruptly turned ninety degrees to the left and south. There the gorge widened slightly, and we hoped there would be more wind to lift the clouds. If not, we could fly farther south until we found a hole in the clouds to get over the hump.

We made the turn and felt a bit of relief. Now, if worse went to worse, we could at least set the helicopter down on a riverbank. The clouds were still low and we peered out the right side of the aircraft looking for an opening. Unexpectedly, the aircraft banked hard to the right and we now skimmed the treetops toward the hump.

Piloting the Squirrel.

Eric said calmly, "I think we can make it." We could see treetops and clouds swirling just high enough that we could see more treetops disappear into the clouds. Then there was nothing. Everything went dark as the clouds engulfed us and monsoon rain pounded the exterior of the chopper.

Erik said, "Watch my GPS and tell me if we get off track." There was a small window by my feet and I watched the bottom of our aircraft literally skim one-hundred foot trees. I replied with a sense of irritation, "What? You watch the fucking trees coming up through our floor!" Sammy slapped my shoulder and with wide bug eyes and frantic hand movements pointed down at the trees that threatened to pull us in. We had just lost seven of our comrades in a helicopter crash in Vietnam in better conditions than this—we should *not* have found ourselves in this position.

Clouds cloaking the mountain.

Eric pulled back on the stick and attempted to gain altitude. As we increased altitude, the mountain still loomed in front of us and the trees appeared as shadows in the mist. I glanced at Erik and his eyes were glued on the GPS and altimeter. He said,

"If I can get to 4,000 feet I think we will be above the highest peak here."

I looked at him to check the level of confidence on his face and asked, "Are you sure?" This was a situation where everything that could have gone wrong did. Now surviving was in the hands of our bush pilot.

"*Pretty* sure," he replied.

The rotors beat heavily in the deluge of water and we slowly went up. The trees finally disappeared from the floor window. Then there was nothing but dark grayness and the pounding of water. Erik watched the altimeter and then slowly pushed the stick forward. Staring intently out the front window, we expected to see a looming mountain or hazy shadow of a large redwood tree materialize out of the thick nothingness in front of us.

After what seemed an eternity, the darkness began to fade. We saw a bit of lighter clouds, a wisp, and finally a window in the haze to take us down the other side of the hump.

* * *

That event was the beginning of a two-year search from hell that would stress and challenge the Lao IE each time we trekked into those mountains. The challenges stacked against us in this area with rugged small mountains, unpredictable weather patterns, long flight distances, and no villages from which to find guides or witnesses. This was a real test of the Investigation Element's determination and abilities. Other teams had come before us and they had left empty handed.

For two years, we had simultaneously investigated two cases on two adjacent small mountains separated by three kilometers and on opposite sides of the Xekong River. This was the mountainous border region of Salavan and Xekong Provinces and host to rugged mountains and terrible weather conditions. In addition, there was another crash site of a fighter plane nearby with no evidence to narrow down the location. With each trip to those mountains we restudied all the historical data, poured over the maps of previous attempts, and tried to find that one shred of evidence that would crack any of those cases.

The first case involved a Green Beret who was aboard a South Vietnamese HH-34 helicopter trying to lower a chainsaw to a Prairie Fire Team. This team consisted of two-hundred South Vietnamese Rangers under attack on the mountaintop. The Green Beret successfully delivered the chainsaw before his helicopter crashed on the side of the mountain. He was never heard from again. We had searched that mountain for two years, up and down, in very disciplined sectors. It was a series of steep drop-offs, ledges, loose rocks and the thickest thorn bushes imaginable. Those sharp thorny vines and bushes would lay in wait to cut open your scalp and exposed skin.

The evidence of the battle was still there with fighting positions, ammunition cans, smoke grenades remnants, and other residue from the battle. We had determined the likely helicopter PZ the team had cut with the chainsaw. From this location we attempted to recreate the battle and estimate the likely location of our lost helicopter.

It was on that mountain that I encountered the biggest snake I had ever seen in the field. I was slowly walking by myself and noticed something moving on the ground to my front. About ten meters in front of me was a huge greenish snake writhing with a smaller blackish snake. This bigger snake was at least eight feet long and as thick as my arm. I moved forward and they detected me approaching. Both snakes bounced off the ground in a flash and disappeared into a bamboo thicket. I was amazed a snake could move that quickly.

Time and again we had trudged up and down those mountains and had found no evidence of the helicopter crash site known to be nearby. Each attempt to locate the site was extremely grueling and the team both embraced the challenge but sensed a state of futility. We knew that without a witness, we could walk within a few meters of the site and never have a clue it was there. In the end, we were missing that one thing you always needed in the jungle—a local guide.

*   *   *

PERSISTENT LUCK

I heard Don Guthrie call over the radio, *"Where are you?"* He circled above the jungle canopy to get better reception from our small hand held radios.

"I'm not sure. We're about halfway down the slope and heading toward the river," I said as I picked my way over a slippery streambed which dropped off below me.

"You guys have got to get out of there. It's getting late and it looks like thunderstorms are coming." He said sternly.

"We're moving!" I said, and we continued to push on. "There were always thunderstorms coming to this area," I muttered to myself.

I could see my two other team members spread out in a loose line as we followed each other down. Our group included me, Adam Pierce, and an EOD augmenter. Greg Parmele was somewhere down below but in radio contact. We had searched this damned mountain so many times. It was littered with drop-offs, cliffs, and impassable vegetation. The weather here along the Vietnam border was always unpredictable. Wind and rain could wash in at any moment and keep us stranded in the "ultimate boonies."

Once we reached the bottom of the slope, the streambed transitioned from slippery rocks to mud and sand. With better footing, we ran ahead until we hit thick grass. You had to protect your face with your hands or the grass would cut you open, leaving thin painful cuts. Then, with no warning, we broke out of the grass and into the open space of a small river about thirty feet wide. We turned left and followed the bank or ran in the water when it was shallow. Soon we popped out of another section of grass along the bank and there was Greg. All together we pushed on. We were drenched with sweat. Clouds of gnats, mosquitoes and horse flies circled our heads.

"Don, we're at the river," I called into my radio.

"I'm on my way." He called back.

We continued to follow the bank and a few minutes later he called back.

"I don't see you. Can you hear the Squirrel?"

I stopped walking and we all listened. We could just make out the sound of his engines and rotors further down river. "Don, come farther upstream."

Don bringing in the extraction bird.

As he rocketed around the corner, he spotted us near the bank. The bright red and white Squirrel rose up above the lowest trees, banked around, and came back down to a hover ten feet above the water. "What in the hell are you guy's doing up here?" he said with a tone of irritation.

I didn't bother to answer and surveyed our possibilities of getting on the Squirrel near our present location. The trees and vegetation were thick and tall and the water looked deep. There was no place to get picked up. "Can you pick us up further down stream?" I said. I held my radio to my mouth with one hand and pointed downstream with the other. Don turned his head, looked at me, and shook his head side to side in the negative. He had been surveying the situation also. "We need to hurry, get into the water, and get onto the skid," he radioed.

The four of us jumped in with our bags held above our heads and waded out until the water was at chin level. Don hovered straight above us and put his skids right on the water. He positioned the left skid closest to us as this allowed him to keep his bodyweight on the opposite side. Balancing the aircraft in gusty winds, while men climbed on the skids, was always risky. We pushed up one team member, handed up the rucksacks, pushed up a second team member, and Don flew away to off load them at the MI-17 parked down stream.

Greg and I stood there up to our necks in water feeling pretty lonely. A few minutes later the Squirrel came rocketing around the corner again. It banked dramatically to the left above the jungle and came down to a hover again. I pushed Greg up and then followed. It was extremely difficult to climb onto a wet skid in heavily soaked clothes. Greg pulled me inside. The river pickup was completed and we headed to the MI-17. The wind chilled me, and I sat shivering as water dripped out of our clothing and soaked the inside of the bird

"You have got to stop doing this," Don said as he glanced over at me through his tinted visor and held up his left index finger to accentuate the point. "You're pushing too hard."

*   *   *

We never did find that helicopter after all the searches we had done—finally we got lucky. By sheer chance, when we arrived at the MI-17, we ran into a Vietnamese fisherman who had sneaked across the border with his son on a day trip. As Don repositioned personnel in the two aircraft, we conducted a quick interview. Luckily, we had a District official with us who spoke Vietnamese. We huddled in a small circle on the water's edge and asked the fisherman if he knew of a crash site on the hill. The fisherman pointed at the hill and shook his head yes. He explained that he had been in the army and had gone to the site previously. To make matters better, he knew of two more crash sites nearby and up river. This immediately correlated to two more sites we were looking for.

This was a complete breach of witness protocol because this was not an official Vietnamese witness. In theory, he had violated the border. After some quick negotiation, the Lao officials agreed to allow the fisherman to guide us to the helicopter on the hill. The other sites would have to wait until after a Tri-Lateral investigation could be arranged between Vietnam, Laos, and the U.S. To find all three sites, in one JFA, would have been too much progress in a short period of time. The Lao always preferred the slow, more profitable, and diplomatically advantageous Tri-lateral process.

Two days later, Greg Parmele went with the Vietnamese fisherman/veteran and found the site. It was right off the trail and fifty feet down a sheer slope. Unfortunately, it was located on the opposite side of the ridgeline from where it was reported to be located. We had walked within thirty meters of that crash site at least ten times over the years. This find was a very big find and the result of an incredible investment in time and energy. We returned two days later and conducted a complete site survey.

All of the major metal parts had been scavenged and taken off the mountain. All that remained was a pile of charred metal and ash. It was common in remote site like this for the scavengers to melt the aluminum down and make it easier to carry. By sifting through the ash and surrounding vegetation we discovered reading glasses, uniform buttons, and personal items. We also found a chainsaw blade like the one the Green Beret Sergeant had attempted to deliver to the troops on the ground. It finally took a stroke of luck to find the right witness to locate that crash site. Now we could get the case to the Recovery Elements. The team was happy we would not have to go on that hill again.

*   *   *

The day before our survey of the helicopter crash site, we sent our 'scoot' team of me, MSG Collins and Greg Parmele up the other hill. We were searching for another Green Beret reported to be fighting from a bomb crater with two other Americans and three local fighters. The team was surrounded and rescue helicopters tried multiple attempts to extract them. Each attempt to hoist out a team member resulted in their being shot in the hoist. The Green Beret we were searching for rose to throw a grenade and was hit in the forehead. The only team member to survive was the last Green Beret who evaded the enemy and was rescued later on. The body of our Green Beret was left behind due to the heavy presence of enemy in the area. All we knew was he was left in a bomb crater near the summit.

We forged hard through the brush, grass, and vines. We reached the top much faster than we had anticipated. Then we had the chain saws lowered in on a rope. We planned to cut a LZ to use over the next two days to search the hilltop with the whole team. We began to cut away and soon we had a hole opened in the canopy. As we expanded it, Don flew up to take a look. He directed us to cut some more on the lead edge. This was not going to be a landing zone. It would have to be another "hovering zone" and he wanted room to maneuver his tail.

I stood on an already fallen tree and completed the last cut on the last tree. As it fell downhill, the tree I stood on shifted and I fell into a straddle position with my foot wedged. The falling tree went away from me and rocked forward on the other fallen trees making the base end rise high into the air. That was when time went into slow motion. That tree was going to come straight down and crush me. I was in such an awkward position that there was no leverage to push myself backwards. As I looked up, I could see that tree was on its way back down. After throwing the chainsaw to the ground I managed to inch myself slightly uphill. In a state of mental and physical fatigue, I resigned myself to the fact that I was going to lose my right leg—if not worse. The tree crashed to a halt with its trunk resting on one of the trees I had just previously cut. I freed myself from the stump and directed we put the saws away. We had pressed our luck for this LZ.

Our team searched along near vertical slopes and located and searched more than eight large bomb craters. A thorough search produced no conclusive evidence. We did find spent 5.56mm shell casings in a crater with a stamped date consistent with the period of the incident. After more searching, we found no other evidence. This mountain would take many days of searching to have any likelihood of finding the correct bomb crater. Even then it was a long shot that the body had not been moved at the time of the incident or over the last thirty-five years. I was certain the Vietnamese from across the border would have the key to this case. We recommended we interview that same fisherman at the earliest opportunity.

Cutting the LZ on the ridgeline.

The sequence of successes we were having were captured in a series of emails I sent home. These excerpts provide insight into the daily efforts of the team. The JFA had started very slowly and with little success. It gained speed as the JFA progressed.

*   *   *

4 Nov:
Today we are going back to the "Land before time!" What a throwback village! Our linguists cannot talk to them and a local official has to translate into Lao. It is a regional and local dialect. Kind of a scary place. National Geographic stuff.

Hopefully, they will hold the key to at least one case and maybe more because they are a mobile society. Wish us luck."

A ridge top landing zone cut in Khammouan province.

8 Nov, 1710 Hrs:

We are now 1/3 through the JFA and I'm smoked right now too. The days have been long and unproductive. This is my 10th JFA; I've lost some of my zest for this mission now. We still do exceptional work but it is work. Today was a bit of a tooth biter. I got stung six times by wasps (left side back, 2 on back of right arm, three on right side of back) and man do they hurt. At least this time it wasn't like Ft. Lewis where I got stung on my head which is very painful. Didn't see their nest and they get you before you even see them - welts all over now.

10 Nov, 0500 Hrs:

Today we have to get to the border and pickup the Vietnamese Delegation coming over for the next week. With luck we can find another couple sites by then. We are still shooting for our 5 site threshold and JFA average.

11 Nov, 1700 Hrs:

Today we went to a site where three witnesses were positive a guy is buried. We dug all afternoon and found nothing. Oh, well.

Hey, tomorrow is the 12th which is a good thing and means we are getting deep into this JFA. I still want to do good work and meet our five aircraft threshold but it is getting harder and harder as each day passes.

12 Nov, 1745 Hrs:

We have just gotten done with our meetings and today was a long, long, day. We were out in the heat and now as a whole we are smoked. The Satellite phone was forgotten in the back of the helicopter so I can't call tonight. I am so tired that may be a good thing because I wouldn't be much good for conversation.

We have to delay our move until the day after tomorrow because our witness thinks he is in the area of the crash we are looking for. Tomorrow I will jump off the skids, cut an LZ and we should be there. Check is in the mail. Heard that one before but it could be our second find of the JFA.

14 Nov, 2128 Hrs

It has been the longest of days and I have just made it back to my room after 'coordination' with the Lao officials. That equates to leaving dinner with the team and being nabbed as I walk by their table to share shots of Lao Lao and informally discuss all the issues at hand. The good thing is they genuinely

*trust and like me and MSG Collins which makes things soooo
much easier for us.*

15 Nov, 0546 Hrs
*Today is the 15th and we are officially half way done and it
needs to get over soon. I woke up at 0400 but couldn't drag
myself out of bed until now. I just stumbled to the desk and
flipped on the computer and started writing. It is safe to say I
am fricken tired.*

16 Nov, 0900 Hrs
*We are in the air and flying to Thakhek. It is a beautiful day
and the flight is 1 hour and 40 minutes. I am taking advantage
of the time to catch up on some report editing.*

*Last night we had our going away dinner with the Salavan
Province officials and the head of the provincial army offered a
toast to the American team. We then were obligated to take a
toast of the moonshine in respect, etc. As it went around, we
speculated what the meaty substance in the bottom of the bottle
was (it was a plastic water bottle). We all agreed it was a
chunk of a snake and some of the guys didn't take that news to
well since they were already done drinking. Then the news got
worse when the Lao told us it wasn't snake but goat balls from
the goat they had killed for dinner. The theory being that goats
breed all the time and the ball will add virility to whoever
drinks it. There were a couple of unhappy folks.*

24 Nov, 0630 Hrs:
*I am just getting moving. Just got my coffee brewed and
have to get ready for a big trek up the hill today. Should take us
about 4 hours in and out which does not include the time at the
site. I'd like to get done with this in time to run over to the site
we have an appt for tomorrow. Potentially our 4th find and 3rd*

helicopter of the JFA. If we find that one this will be a monumental JFA. It will add up to 14 servicemen located in one JFA!!! Wish us luck for the next 48 hours.

24 Nov, 2100 Hrs:

We walked down a streambed today because our guide got lost. I knew where we were and was familiar with the area but because we were on the way out I walk towards the rear to make sure no one gets left behind. By the time I saw what had happened it was too late. We had gone off a ridgeline and into a stream. Moss covered slippery rocks. We all had our spills and I had two bad ones. The first fall I fell and went completely under and came up swimming. The Doc was laughing so hard he couldn't even walk for a while. The second was when I was giving our guide grief for getting us into that hole. My feet went out from under me and I went flat on my back into the rocks. Bounced of the rocks in a rapids and finally came up in a foul mood. It will be a Motrin night tonight.

26 Nov, 1900 Hrs:

Just got done with dinner. We had spaghetti night tonight. Everyone digs deep into their food boxes and dig out whatever is left to add to the sauce and make common dinner. It was pretty good and we had a beer together.

Today we surveyed two crash sites today. The last village we went to this old village chief made us come into his hut and he broke out the Lao Lao (rice moonshine). I had three full shots because I am the leader and the other guys had about the same. The chief also served wild pig jerky and boiled eggs and rice. It was pretty cool and the chief loved it.

27 Nov, 0610 Hrs:

Got up a few minutes ago because I stayed up late last night working on reports. Now, my first cup of coffee is brewed and I finished another bag of Starbuck's coffee. It is such an awesome treat out here; much thanks for getting it for me.

We are pushing ahead with two cases today, one tomorrow and one the next day and that will be the end. 22 of 22 cases investigated. At this point, 17 servicemen accounted for by this IE (16 for sure and 1 to be determined). It would be cool to find another before we leave but almost too much to hope for. I am so proud of what we have done. The last trip we found six crash sites and accounted for 6. This trip we found five and accounted for 17!

*　　*　　*

The search for the Jolly Green Giant was a long and arduous affair. On January 28, 1970, a HH-53 "Jolly Green Giant" helicopter was lost with six crewmembers on board. It had been in the process of aerial refueling, at an altitude of 7,000 feet, when a MiG fighter jet hit it with an air-to-air missile. The helicopter broke into two parts and crashed into the jungle along the Vietnam/Laos border.

The site was located in a remote mountainous region in northeastern Khammouan Province. The weather in that area was frequently cloudy and rainy. Any clear days brought gusting and swirling winds. It was extremely rugged with thick jungle canopy throughout. To complicate things, there were no villages within twelve miles of the record loss location and no natural clearings to use as a landing zone.

This search began on my first mission as Team Leader to Laos. We started by staging fuel barrels and pumps at the village twelve miles away. There was a small border post located there and we paid the guards to secure our fuel. From there we took the Squirrel and flew for hours over the area in an attempt to find a place to land and get the team on the ground near the record loss location.

Finally Bruce, a Kiwi bush pilot, spotted an opening in the trees at the junction of two large streams. He slowly descended the Squirrel under the upper canopy of branches. Then he carefully backed the bird under the trees to a sand bar on the edge of the stream. We jumped out with machetes and hatches and cleared the residue to create the best LZ we could muster. As long as he kept his tail boom over water, we were O.K. This LZ would serve us for the next three years.

The remainder of the team ferried in and then began a single file trek up the mountain to the north on a steep grade through the jungle. Within fifteen minutes we had two sick members and were near mutiny. I brought Gunny Carabello to the front and told him to just keep bringing the team up the ridge until they got to flat ground. When they reached the top, they could take an extended rest stop. I would push ahead and walk the ridgeline to scout for wreckage. Gunny thought I expected too much from the team, but I felt the team needed to raise their game ... bring out their "A" game.

On the way up the hill, I found a small utility door that looked to be from a helicopter. That door was a bit of evidence that would both help and haunt us over the next three years. After surging up the hill, I started to walk the flat area of the large ridgeline. I hoped to find more wreckage or evidence of metal scavenging. It was normal for metal scavengers to pile the wreckage by the side of the trail to be picked up later.

After another 500 meters there was nothing but I decided to go just a bit further. It was at that time that I started thinking of my Long Range Surveillance Leader Course and how to avoid booby traps on the trails. I imagined being the point man of a recon team during the war and moving down this ridgeline. After cresting one last knoll, I stopped, turned around and intended to hustle back to the team. The team had just radioed informing he they had reached the top of the ridge.

After just two or three steps I fell to the ground, flat on my face. I tried to stand up but my foot was being pulled. After a closer look, I could see a cable around the center of my foot. It ran under a log and up into a tree. The tree had been bent over and was now trying to straighten back up. I had been snared!

I called on the radio and said, *"You won't believe what just ..."*
Gunny's' voice cut in, *"break, break, Sir, Sammy just got caught in a trap!"*

I pulled the cable, got some slack, and removed it from my foot. It was pretty ingenious. The tree bent down, cable run under the log, hooked on the stout stick, and looped around the hole. When a large animal (or me) came along, stepped in the hole, and broke the stick, the tree drew the loop around the foot or leg. It was far superior to anything I had done as a kid trapping back on the farm in Iowa.

I freed myself and ran down the ridge to the remainder of the team to see how they were doing. When I got back, Gunny told me the story. Apparently, Sammy got caught in a snare like I did and didn't know what was happening. He was on his backside and frantically trying to pull backward and screaming like a wounded animal. Another team member yelled at him that it was a trap. Master Sergeant Clifford thought they meant "trap" as in ambush. He started to run down the hill to get away. He explained later that if we were taken prisoner, someone had to get away to tell the story. Sammy was clearly shaken and the Lao officials were very concerned.

The officials had often warned of monkey traps that utilized a poison dart. When the monkey went for the bait, the dart would shoot into their flesh. When the monkey realized he had been hit with the poison, he would actually just sit and cry. Apparently, they could identify the poison and know they were going to die. The officials were serious in their fear and concern for these traps. I did not openly discount the existence of these type traps but also did not take them seriously.

After a short rest we got over the trap trauma and continued our search. We searched the eastern slope of that ridgeline for the next three days and found nothing to suggest the helicopter was nearby. It was a very rough search as the terrain consisted of deep vertical ravines covered by triple canopy jungle. It was extremely difficult to maintain a line search or navigate the side of the mountain.

We searched that ridge for many days over three JFAs to no avail. At that point, I had decided we needed to walk the ridgelines in the area. Hopefully, we could locate a wreckage pile to let us know we were close. There were two more ridgelines, like the one we were on, within two kilometers to the west. That crash site was somewhere nearby.

In this case the whole investigation system came together to provide success. Interviews had taken place in Vietnam, which had identified a trapper who knew of a site on our side of the border. During my trip to Vietnam, I had the opportunity to talk with him. From his description I had sketched a map which had driven our search.

MSgt Rex Hodges inspecting wreckage of the "Jolly Green"

During that next JFA, we got lucky and the Vietnamese trapper came to Laos as part of a Tri-lateral investigation. He would lead us to the site if he could. During his interview he described the area where he had found a crash site and drew us a crude sketch. In his sketch he described the junction of two streams where he had camped and two very large trees nearby. I asked how big the trees were and he said two men could not put their arms around them. In those trees he had carved a likeness of Ho Chi Minh into one and a likeness of Lenin into the other—facing each other. He said from that location he could walk us to the site.

SSG Whitfield surveying the wreckage field.

A few days later we had him in the Squirrel and we landed at the same stream junction we had used two years earlier. We walked him up to a small campsite we had seen there, and he said it was the spot. I was unconvinced and asked him where the trees were and the carvings. He walked me over to two trees

117

and pointed. I looked at the trees and saw no carvings. I held up my hands as if to say, "Nothing here!" He smiled, grunted, and motioned for me to look on the other side. I pushed a big frond fern out of the way and there it was. I could make out the old curvature of the head and a pointy chin carved on the tree. It was a surreal moment that after two years we had been standing right next to the biggest clue and never knew—like Indiana Jones looking for the Ark of the Covenant.

Tri-lat investigation: (left to right); VN official, LTjg Eric Castillo (backwards hat), Sammy (sitting), MSG Collins (green cap),VN witness Mr. Nguyan Minhe Le, SSG Pierce (kneeling) , me in the back, Lao Official, SSG Brian Eamin (white hat), SSG Eathan Whitfield, Reggie Mathis (blue cap, and Lao Official).

The next day the VN trapper led us up a r.
straight to the site. It was two ridgelines to the we
four kilometers away. That was another *Holy Grail*
success that involved all of JTF-FA from Hawaii, Vie ...n, and
Laos and the Lao and Vietnam POW/MIA contingents.

To our team's credit, we would have found it that JFA with
or without him but it was no matter. We found the crash site,
which consisted of burnt metal and wreckage spread over a
large area. We recommended the site for excavation and knew
the Excavation Team would have to do a wide search. It was
the last Jolly Green Giant missing in SEA and hopefully the
resulting excavation would get its crew back home.

Lao and U.S. combined team photo.

THICK LUCK

*   *   *

The team experienced many hazards, including extremely difficult terrain, hot and humid temperatures, unexploded ordnance, spiders and leeches, and the unknown. On an investigation in Attapu province, Pierce, Sammy, myself, and a Lao official were jumping from village to village looking for a witness to find a jet crash site along the Vietnam/Laos border. A young man told us of a site where two airplanes had crashed on a nearby hill. After some clarifying questions we learned that two helicopters had likely crashed on the hilltop. We were not immediately excited about the possible find because we were focused on finding a jet crash site. We accepted the young man's invitation to be led to the site and made an appointment to arrive early the next morning. The young man agreed to trek to the site with some other villagers and cut a landing zone for us to land in the next day.

When we arrived we found the wreckage of two burned out HH-53 helicopters sitting inside a dense area of jungle. Fighting positions and rusted weapons and TA-50 were spread throughout the area. We inspected the site and collected aircraft part numbers for evidence. I looked up, told Sammy not to move, and flicked a leech off his shirt. After I flicked another and another, I suggested we take a look around. The ground was moving with leeches!

This was a good find and we later determined it had not been found previously. There had been a Green Beret advisor to the South Vietnamese Army onboard and attempting to extract South Vietnamese infantry fighting from that hilltop. The helicopter was shot down and rolled and burst into flame before the advisor could jump clear. We had found another missing crash site by casing the area. We were operating in the most southern province of Laos so this site would not be excavated for a number of years due to the north to south progression of excavations.

M60 door-gun left in the wreckage of the HH-34's.

We often discussed what made these leeches so hearty. No one could agree if they felt the vibration of you walking, sensed your heat, or sensed your breath. Somehow they sensed your presence and actually walked toward you on the ground or jumped on you from the trees and bushes.

It became pretty much a standard operating procedure to tape around the top of our boots with duct tape to keep the leaches from getting in. Leaches could get in even the smallest openings in your clothes and they came from the ground or vegetation. In a case when we stopped to rest, we would only sit in one place for a couple minutes and then move again. Otherwise, the leaches would search you out.

Remnants of the HH-34 helicopters in a leech invested grove.

On another occasion, Sammy and I were in an interview on a village chief's porch. Sammy stopped talking, started scratching his leg and jumped up. He dropped his pants right in the interview and out rolled a big fat green blood filled leech. The chief's wife just laughed and Sammy pulled up his pants and kept on talking. It was very common for a leech to unknowingly attach itself to you and fill itself up with blood and drop off later. There would be trails of blood in the aircraft as they tried to crawl away.

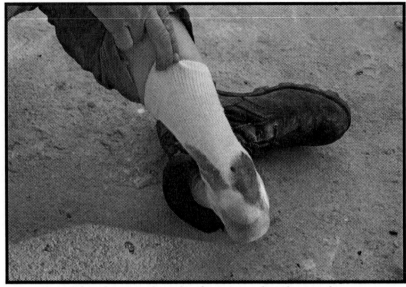

Blood stained sock after a two leach attack.

Up early for breakfast, I walked into the team room at a small hotel we were staying at and was taken aback. There, shirtless and bent over the table was our EOD technician. Doc stood over him from behind. I asked, "Uh, what's going on?" not really wanting to know. It turned out a big leech bite had been draining for days on the lower back of the technician. The Doc was trying to cauterize it with some acid - those leeches were bad.

*   *   *

We returned to the same village where I hurt my eye in 2001. On this second visit, we were to determine if there was more than one crash site in the area. In the mid-1990s, a team had visited the village and witnesses had reported a crash site with life support items. They couldn't approach the site due to all the UXO in the area which included cluster munitions and BLU-43 Dragon tooth anti-personnel mines. Therefore, they sent a villager into the site that came out with helmet parts. This report was not consistent with the report filed on my first trip. Now we were going back to determine if there were actually two sites and not just one.

We did our homework and received a class on the BLU-43. Apparently, it was an all-plastic air-scattered anti-personnel mine that was almost totally undetectable. It was green and smaller than the size of your hand with little wings.

We returned to the village and quizzed the village chief about the crash site on the edge of the village. He said it was the same site, but the village had done its own UXO removal. It wasn't very scientific, but they just picked the mines up and moved them out.

The team went back to the same area where I had hurt my eye a year earlier. It was now different because more brush had been cleared for pasture area. There were the cluster munitions again. As we searched, MSG Collins found a piece of parachute so I went over and we searched a small area near a tree. He kept following the line of the parachute and I started digging a bit further in that direction. I noticed that there was a little open area in the base of the tree. Cluster munitions were stacked in it to keep them out of the way.

As I dug, I found a survival knife blade and other items that the pilot would have been carrying. That was when another team member, I think MSG Collins said, "Hey! Look at this."

He started to throw his discovery as I started to say, "Don't throw ..." and it was in the air.

Wreckage indicated more than one crash site was nearby.

There sailed a BLU-43 on its way to the Explosive Ordnance Expert's outstretched hand. It was a moment that everything went into slow motion. The Expert went for it, thankfully caught it with no big bang and said, "Hey, that's a BLU-43."

After a piece of ordnance or wreckage goes through a crash, heat and thirty years in the ground, it just doesn't look the same. You *always* had to be on your game. This mine looked like a bent tootsie roll the size of your little finger with the wings not pronounced. We were lucky.

The evidence we found on that survey correlated the crash site and indicated at least one crew member was in the aircraft at the time of impact. It was another success.

Clues to the type of aircraft in the nearby jungle.

Chapter 5
Big Challenges

In July 2002, Lieutenant Colonel Kevin Smith, the Detachment 3 Commander, requested I return to Houaphan Province and try to pinpoint the gravesite of Earthquake McGoon. This case had been investigated two years earlier and a site was specified for excavation. When the DET3 Commander went to the area to prepare it for excavation, he could not find any evidence of a crash site. Therefore, he asked that I be sent along with a Vietnam analyst to reinvestigate the case.

James B. McGovern was a soldier of fortune who flew for the CIA in Southeast Asia. He was a WWII pilot with nine confirmed kills to his credit. He was a larger than life personality at six feet tall, 260 pounds and was nicknamed after the 'Earthquake McGoon' cartoon character created by Al Capp. During a resupply mission for the besieged French garrison at Bien den phu, Vietnam, his Air America C-119 cargo plane was hit by ground fire. His tail rudder was damaged and he nursed his aircraft into northern Laos before crashing. Both the pilot and co-pilot were killed on impact. What became of Earthquake McGoon and Wally Buford became a mystery of great speculation.

Witnesses had provided statements that they had observed the body of a large white man at the crash site. No witness had been located who had knowledge of where the bodies were taken or buried. Books were written which suggested their remains had been removed to a shrine in a nearby village.

James B. McGovern and his co-pilot, Wallace A. Buford,
crashed in northern Laos on May 6, 1954. (courtesy POW/MIA
Network)

In 2002, George Bush senior, at the request of the McGovern family, applied political pressure to find and recover Earthquake's remains. James McGovern's mother was becoming quite elderly and her sons hoped to bring resolution to the case. That was our big challenge—locate the remains of Earthquake McGoon and Wally Buford.

We met with three Lao village elders the previous team had used as the basis of their investigation. Statements from these witnesses led to a recommendation to excavate a site near the stump of a large old tree. The previous team determined the C-119 had hit this tree and then broken apart. We accompanied the witnesses to this site and determined their information about the crash was not conclusive. Due to their advanced age it was possible their memories could have faded over time. Therefore, we continued with interviews at every village in the area. We extended this interview process to the district capitals to the east and west of the crash site. This effort provided no new witnesses or tangible information.

After covering 75 miles and approaching 4,000-foot mountains Earthquake made a last radio transmission and his C-119 plowed into a Laotian hillside. (Courtesy POW Network)

After three days of investigation, we learned little to help bring resolution to this case. We did make use of the metal detectors to map the edge of the old crash site. We also learned from a local lady that a specific portion of the road was considered haunted. The local children to this day would run by this stretch of road after dark. They believed this was the place where the ghosts lurked.

Children that would run passed the ghosts.

We compared historical photos of the crash site, which appeared in *Life Magazine* to the river and existing road. This comparison narrowed our search area down to a few hundred meters in length. Lastly, we compared a narrative and sketch provided from the previous team's findings. This comparison extended our search area 300 meters in length. We then tried to identify trends in the witness testimony. If multiple unrelated witnesses identified a similar location then we could begin to narrow the search area. Finally, we exhausted our witness base by interviewing three elderly male local villagers. They had been in the area during the time of the crash but not at the crash site. They claimed to have seen dirt piles they believed were graves. They pointed out a fifty meter area along the road and said the grave would be within three steps of the road.

We finally got lucky after interviews in two villages we had initially bypassed because they were set back a few miles from the road. A Lao elder had just arrived from Vientiane to arrange the funeral of his nephew. He claimed to know the exact spot the American was buried. The location he pointed to coincided with the spot identified by the other three male elders. Their combined information narrowed our site down to a thirty meter long by ten meter wide area along the road. This spot was one-hundred meters from the site identified by the previous team.

It was also consistent with speculation that the road had changed. Dirt had been taken from one side and used to expand and raise the roadbed. With this expansion, it was rumored the grave was now under the edge of the road. There would be no conclusive physical proof. Our recommendation would be based on a combination of first and second hand witness statements along with local folklore. That was the basis of our recommendation. We were directed not to come home without the gravesite located—we had identified a gravesite for Earth Quake McGoon and Wally Buford.

Mapping the wreckage field of the "Box Car"

The site was excavated by a team from CILHI on the next Joint Field Activity in Laos. In true anthropological fashion, they did not start digging where we had said. They started at the furthest edge of the recommended site and worked along the road. On the last day, in the last grid to be dug, they found a full set of very large skeletal remains. Later testing would need to be conducted at CILHI to compare DNA to the McGoon and Buford families.

"Ghost Road" in northern Laos.

The HistoryNet.com, Editorial June 2003,
(*http://historynet.com/vn/editorial_06_03/*)

*On December 7, 2002, Stars and Stripes reported that several sets of human remains from Laos had been returned to American soil two days earlier. The identification process may take months, but it is possible that Wally Buford and Earthquake McGoon have finally come home. -- **D.T.Z.***

*　　*　　*

A t the Ban Alang Base Camp, I was introduced to Earl Swift by LTC Kevin Smith, the Detachment 3 Commander. Earl was a reporter who was writing a book on the excavation of a helicopter which crashed during the Lom San Offensive in 1971. This offensive involved South Vietnamese ground troops supported and inserted by U.S. aircraft and pilots. This case had involved the loss of an entire aircraft and crew as it tried to evacuate South Vietnamese infantry that were surrounded by North Vietnamese regulars.

The American pilots flew hundreds of harrowing sorties in an attempt to bring out those South Vietnamese soldiers. The result was the loss of 168 U.S. helicopters. In this incident, a crew had successfully flown into LZ Brown. On departing from the plateau top LZ, the helicopter was hit by ground fire, crashed on the valley floor, and burst into flame. It was witnessed by other aircraft but no search and rescue successfully reached the crash site

We were the third team to investigate the record loss area. We surveyed three helicopter crash sites, within a few hundred meter radius, and attempted to differentiate between the aircraft. We then recommended one site for excavation based on witness statements from a farmer. The weathered old farmer claimed to have seen uniform pieces and a flight helmet at this crash site. He pulled the flight helmet from his hut and held if up for all to see. It was a weathered flight helmet with a bullet hole running through it. He said for years he had worn the helmet while working in the field to keep the sun off his head.

Earl Swift having the Lao Lao experience during an interview.

He guided us to that site and we searched it extensively. It consisted of a bomb crater adjacent to an intermittent streambed. Pig and goat trails ran around the rim of the bomb crater. The remainder of the area was overgrown with thick underbrush and small trees. We surveyed the site and found metal and small aircraft parts consistent with a U.S. helicopter. This site matched the record loss grid of the aircraft in question. Based on these facts, I thought we had the right location.

Earl accompanied the Recovery Element during the excavation of the crash site. It was an extensive excavation which culminated in failure. After weeks of work, the excavation team found a data plate, which I thought correlated with an operational loss aircraft. This was one of the other aircraft shot down during the extraction effort on the top of the mountain. Earl chronicled an expensive effort which proved my recommendation was wrong. His book is titled, *Where they Lay*.

LTC Smith asked me to take Earl with us during a day of investigations so he could see how we operated. I agreed with some apprehension and LTC Smith stopped me. He glared at me and said, "Dave, take it easy on him … he is a good guy!"

The next day we flew to a ridgeline about the base camp where he had been searching unsuccessfully for an F-4 Phantom jet. There were a string of small villages atop the ridgeline and we intended to stop and interview at every one of them until we got a lead.

Helmet from a helicopter pilot later confirmed as rescued.

By the end of the interviews we had been shown various evidence to include a pilots' helmet. We were also guided to a crash site which correlated to an Operational Loss.

Then we made plans to visit a record loss site in a remote valley that no team had previously confirmed was an Operational Loss. The foot movement would be quite short if we could get our helicopters into a small clearing atop the ridgeline. Then it would be a half-mile trek down through the jungle into the low ground. Low ground meant cooler temperatures but large amounts of insects, thick brush, and vines to contend with.

Two Squirrels in a small LZ on a rainy day.

We successfully got on the ground and started our downward trek. It was somewhat slippery in the steep trail cut by the guide we had brought along. The further down we went the cooler it became but the humidity and sweat soaked our clothing in short order. We reached the creek bed at the bottom and a short time later the Lao guide had found the wreckage.

Wreckage of an airplane in the remote stream bed.

We searched through the brush along the creek and found bits of wreckage which were pretty much useless. It became apparent that any of the larger aluminum parts had been taken away by local scavengers for sale to the metals buyers. The pieces that were left were heavy and stuck in the mud. Rudy Alvarez and I pried a large chunk of engine from the muck and shook it in the water to wash away the mud. The result of our labor was some parts numbers which would likely indicate this aircraft was not what we were looking for.

Then it was time to climb back to the helicopters and head to another village for interviews. The climb up was more difficult than the slip and slide that had gotten us to the bottom. Now we were pulling on branches and using bursts of energy to get by greasy spots in the wet clay soil. It was hot and it created a sense of stress in the group. I liked these physical challenges because it was truly a challenge between some of the team members, some Lao officials and our guides. The guides did not like to get out hiked and we pushed them hard.

Wreckage after it was washed in the creek.

The guys in the back of the column had the hardest time because the trail was made more slippery from the guys up front. They worked much harder and that's where Earl was – in the back. The front of the group got to the Squirrels and took off our shirts to cool down. Later on, Rudy Alvarez and Earl reached the LZ. Earl was tired and took some time to cool down. He had gotten a small dose of what we potentially experienced everyday.

Marine SGT Rudy Alvarez surveying the crash site.

Earl had made the comment in his book that my Investigation Team was aloof and we considered ourselves cowboys. This assessment was somewhat accurate as we did spend time by ourselves. This was a product of the work we were doing and the experiences that we shared. Each day was another set of dangerous visits to remote locations. We consistently sparred with witnesses, officials, and the environment. We did not know what each day held in store for us—we had to remain mentally prepared.

*   *   *

Many times I would tell the team it should be an easy day. As the day progressed we would be trekking up steep mountain trails and laboring in the sun and heat. On other days, I would tell the team it was going to be a "ball buster." Everyone would have a game face on only to find out we could not do what we had planned. The team would then wait for hours in a village or back of the aircraft. It was always painful to pass the time during slow periods due to weather or witness delays.

We maintained a very physically strong core of team members. I worked with the EOD and Medical sections to ensure we had the most physically fit augmenters to fill out the team. It was a necessity because we had to ensure we could reach remote locations and get out within the same day. If we were unlucky enough to have an injury, we would have a severe problem of getting the casualty out of the remote jungle. There was no one coming to help us—we had to fend for ourselves. Even at the base camps at 0500 hours, under a poorly lighted grass thatched canopy, we would be lifting weights and attempting to stay strong. We didn't run much in country, because the strain of the treks up the mountain kept our legs in great shape. We had to stay strong and fit for forty days in the jungle. At the same time, we never knew what each day would bring.

Our plan for the most extreme circumstance was to lower chain saws and survival stores via a rope to the team on the ground. The team could then cut a location for an extraction to take place. If that failed, the team would have to carry the injured guy out on a poncho litter. Our investigations were fluid and emerging sites unplanned. Often we happened upon a crash site during normal investigations. We could trek to a remote site that no one other than our team and pilots would be aware of. No search and rescue was coming. This fact was sobering as we considered the remoteness of our operations.

Our techniques for remote sites were unorthodox and not advertised outside the team. The pilot removed the right door and seat cushions from the Squirrel. Then we would fly to the desired insertion area, to look for a suitable tree or clearing near our goal. If it were a tree, I would climb down onto the skid, grab it with both hands, and then hang downward. Depending on the situation, I would make a decision to either jump to the ground or be lowered into the tree. I would then climb down to the ground to wait for the lowering of the saws. I never let another team member go first. I always led the team out of the aircraft to ensure that if someone was hurt or stranded it would be me.

The first time I tried this technique was on a mountaintop in Khammouan Province, along the Vietnam/Laos border. The mountaintop was generally flat and covered with a huge area of solid jungle canopy. This was a Trilateral Investigation and a Vietnamese woodcutter was looking out the right side of the aircraft and giving directions. After about twenty minutes he excitedly pointed at the ground. There was a very small clearing and we could see a white aircraft landing strut. It was clearly visible against a small bedrock cliff face. I planned to drop in off the skid and cut the small trees with my Gerber hatchet. The helicopter and the remainder of the team and witnesses would then land.

As I hung from the skid, it became apparent that the trees were much taller than expected. The Squirrel could not get any lower and I could not get back on the skid. Therefore, I got my feet on the top of a tree and just let go. As I descended, my feet hit thicker and thicker branches as I grasped for a handhold.

The branches slowed my fall and I ended up sitting on the ground. I sat there, wiggled each of my limbs, and found I was none the worse for wear. As I looked up at the open door of the Squirrel hovering over me I could see Sammy's head peaking over the edge of the seat. He waved at me as if to say, "Your on you own—I'm not coming down there!"

We grew comfortable with using the "skid drop" technique and successfully located sites previously considered out of reach. The Lao West Coast pilots seemed to look for opportunities to get me on the skid. Trees, high grass, karsts, cliffs, rivers and streams. They seemed to enjoy the challenge.

*   *   *

Chapter 6
The Bone Hunters

On 14 August 2001, the team interviewed at the village of called Ban Larou Saria along the Vietnam/Laos border. We were looking for an aircraft crash site. The villagers had told a local official of a mountainside crash site close to their village and requested he bring the "bone hunters."

We had developed a reputation with the locals as we flew over their villages during our operations. Whenever we stopped at any village, we were always looking for the bones of our comrades. Word had spread amongst the locals and when they saw the red and white helicopters they knew the bone hunters were on the prowl.

The Investigation Team using a river to avoid thick jungle.

Often we would encounter hunters, fisherman, and tree cutters deep in remote jungles during our searches. They would stop to talk to us and wonder how we had found our way deep into the mountains. The Lao always considered us a great mystery. *Why would these men work so hard to find old bones?* We explained we were not after "bones." We were looking for our lost soldiers.

We loaded two villagers in the helicopter and did an aerial recon of the mountain. The pilot explained that the top of the narrow ridgeline was the border between Vietnam and Laos. He said we needed to be careful since the Vietnamese were extremely sensitive about any minor violation of the border by helicopters. Therefore, our approach and departure would be extremely hampered when dealing with the winds coming off the Gulf of Tonkin.

As we scouted the area, the Lao witness in the back seat pointed animatedly at a small clearing with a lone, dead and sun bleached trunk of a tree still standing. That was a reference point he was familiar with.

Steffen, the pilot, said, "I think I can put you right in the top of that tree,"

I replied, "Really … that tree looks over twenty-feet tall."

"Yeah. I can put you in the top and you can climb down."

I eyed him to see if he was joking, "Uh huh, I think you just want see me stuck in the top of that tree! My luck the branch will break."

Steffen replied in his New Zealand English drawl, "Aw c'mon, don't be all whingy about it!"

With a grin on my face I replied, "I tell you what. The grass doesn't look that tall. Try to hover down and I'll drop off the skid and cut an LZ with my machete." My machete was a wicked weapon. I spent countless hours pondering the next day's trek of the mountains, while honing the edge with a sharpening stone. It was always sharp enough to shave with.

Steffen maneuvered in, I hung from the skid, and dropped much further down than I had expected—it was always that way. It also always hurt as you did a perfect airborne landing fall (PLF) to reduce the impact. Your body hit feet, knees, butt, shoulder and then head covered by your arms. In short fashion, we had a small LZ cut to land the helo.

The two witnesses moved down the ridge and searched for about an hour with no luck. This was a time where patience was everything and we sat under the jungle canopy to get out of the hot sun. To be in the shade is always better. The problem is the insects and critters also head to the shade to avoid the sun. There were always bees, flies, and leaches - big bees and flies - little bees and flies - and more leaches.

The witnesses came back and said they could not find the crash site by starting from the top of the mountain. However, they were certain they could find it if they started from the bottom. I was skeptical, and a witness must have seen the doubt on my face. He then pointed at his boot laces made out of parachute string and smiled. I felt more confident with a bit of evidence. We then made plans for the next day to start from the bottom and walk up.

The next day, three witnesses led the team up a streambed headed toward the east and Vietnam. The terrain abruptly turned very steep and we started our ascent. Streambeds were good because they offered a generally clear path. They also had a stair step of vertical drop-offs to climb over.

Helping the next man over the slippery rocks.

We lost two team members when a large rock came loose. The team medic fell and hurt his leg. I sent him back down the slope with Rex to the helo to wait for us. Rex was our JTF-FA Life Support Technician for this trip. Rex was a big man standing around six foot six inches and weighing at least 250 pounds. Rex was a workhorse on dry ground but for some reason the wet and moss covered rocks in the streambeds were his nemesis. His entire left leg from the knee down turned completely black and blue after numerous falls onto the rocks.

Rex taking a break deep in the jungle.

The remainder of the team pushed straight up a very steep incline for around three hours. It was grueling and draining in the heat of the day and we were drenched in sweat. Many times you would take one step up and slide two steps back. It was a tough climb.

SGT Rudy Alvarez had accepted the challenge to see if he could keep up with the team. He had a way of always making things competitive. As we pushed up the steep slope, I would turn to see Rudy red-faced from struggling under the weight of his rucksack. He was digging deep inside himself to ensure the old Ranger did not embarrass the young Marine.

Finally we reached the area where the crash site was thought to be located. A Lao guide gave the familiar whoop to let us know he found the site. He then clanged his machete on metal wreckage to prove his point.

The crash site consisted of a fifteen by twenty foot hole in the side of the very steep ridgeline. There were numerous pieces of small wreckage and a trail of metal dispersed down the hill. We searched the site and found long strips of film from a nose camera, parachute pieces, and a large piece of aluminum with a data plate on it.

That night we sent the information back to Hawaii and Bill Forsythe contacted a manufacturer in California. It turned out we had discovered the crash site of a drone that had been on its way into Vietnam. It did not clear the top of the ridgeline and never came home.

*   *   *

For over a year we had searched for a Navy A-6 jet in Savannakhet Province. During a two ship bombing run in Laos, the wingman lost contact with the missing aircraft. The missing pilot was in the lead and the surviving aircraft followed behind. The surviving crew returned to their ship but the lead aircraft never returned. Upon debrief, the surviving crew remembered the flash of an explosion along the flight route. This could have been the missing aircraft exploding and became the basis for the record loss location. That record loss location had driven our investigation to this point.

During the investigation in Xekong and Salavan Provinces, we stopped at a village where the locals had information on multiple crash sites in the area. They knew of one to the west, one to the east, one on the mountain to the south, and another "up there." The village chief stood and pointed to the top of a mountain range towering 5,000 feet above his village. We asked him if he had told other American teams about this site on the mountain. He confirmed he had. He said when he pointed it out to the other teams they looked at the mountain, shook their heads, and then flew away. He suspected the crash site was too hard for them to reach.

We interviewed other witnesses at a neighboring village. They explained that the crash site was right on the boundary between the two villages. Therefore, we would have to take guides from both villages if we wanted to visit the site.

It was also determined the crash site consisted of a lot of metal, many big bombs, and cloth. The aircraft apparently hit the top of the mountain and then slid down into a swamp. We compared this information to our data base of known aircraft losses and found nothing. Whatever was up there was not supposed to be there. The village chief and I boarded the

Squirrel and we flew to the top of the mountain. Right on the top of the ridgeline we could make out the scarring in the jungle canopy. Old trees had been knocked down and a dark green strip of shorter and thicker vegetation was easy to recognize.

Mountain mist over the village.

We then tried to locate a landing zone close enough to the summit to allow us to reach the site in one day. We would have to ascend to the crash site and return down the mountain before dark. We located a rocky hilltop on the ridgeline about one-third of the way up. We then made plans to ascend the ridgeline later in the week. The weather was unpredictable on that mountain and clouds regularly masked the summit. We had to have a good plan, a good weather day, and some luck to get it done safely.

Don Guthrie was our pilot again. He was experienced and knew the weather and air currents around these mountains. Calm weather on one side could be greeted with a wind sheer around the next corner. Conditions were very tricky and varied by season. In this case, the top of this mountain would be accessible only a few months out of the year.

On mission day, we successfully inserted onto the hilltop and moved up into the clouds to reach the site. It was a heavy misty day on the mountain and we moved fast to complete our mission. By the time we reached the site, much of the team was already tired but we executed a good search. As promised, there was a lot of metal, bombs, and other wreckage. The swamp turned out to be a wet area just fifteen meters down from a small knoll on the ridgeline.

I dug down between the gnarled roots of small trees and quickly discovered harness webbing. Already we had evidence a crew was in the aircraft at the time of impact. Next, we located and identified the type of bombs. This weapons payload data could be critical to identify the type of aircraft. Pierce then yelled that he had found pieces of the tail section with painted numbers on them. From these pieces we extracted three total digits - two from opposite sides and one common digit. We conducted a quick site survey for future excavation. About this time Don hovered several thousand feet below and told us to get the hell out of there because the weather was going to shit.

The Lao official felt they knew a better route down the mountain that involved intersecting an old Vietnamese trail used during the war. I agreed with some reservation. An alternate route meant we would travel in a direction that I had no knowledge of. This could be a recipe for disaster.

We began movement and I pulled up the rear of the line of team members moving through a dark, misty, murky, driving rain. After fifteen minutes, we were right back where we started, and I was questioning the logic of following the local guide. He reassured the linguists we were okay so we began a long, winding two-hour descent down the mountain.

After about an hour, we found the Vietnamese trail, which still had ammo cans and other debris from the war. We followed the trail. Every so often Don would fly below us telling us to hurry up and get below the cloud line.

Aircraft numbers on the unidentified aircraft's wreckage.

This was a memorable movement because it was the first time I can remember that Pierce had felt bad. He said he had cramps and was feeling lousy. I chided him and told him I would tell everyone he was whining like a girl if he fell out. He didn't, and we moved down the mountain.

We finally dropped below the clouds and made our way out on a long ridgeline that we had seen from the air. It was laden with ten-foot tall grass and had some large dead fir trees spaced upon it. We now needed to find a spot where we could cut a pick-up zone the Squirrel could use to pick us up. We began cutting when Don flew by and told us to move another two-hundred meters down the ridge. We complied and cut the grass to a level where Don could hover. We loaded three men per lift to get them out. After they were loaded, the Squirrel would fight the buffeting winds and dive over the edge of the incline to gain lift from the added speed. We repeated this four times until the last lift when Don said we had to get everyone on board because the weather was going to shit again. I told him all we had left were 'heavy drops' (heavy guys over two hundred pounds). He said we had to go for it. We loaded the four heavy drops, plummeted over the edge of the ridge to gain speed, and flew away as the clouds washed over the area again.

Once back at the base camp, we plugged the tail number digits into a database and did a search of all missing aircraft in Laos. A comparison of the tail numbers gave a match to one possible aircraft and set of circumstances.

Circumstances of loss (courtesy POW/MIA Network):
On 22 November 1969, the two-man crew of an A-6A aircraft were part of a two ship night armed reconnaissance mission against trucks on routed 922 and 92 using airborne moving target identification radar. The two aircraft were spaced approximately ten minutes apart with the case aircraft in the lead and his wingman in trail. While making his run, the wingman observed a large explosion and fire at his 10 o'clock position and passed with the fire on his left (west). The fireball quickly subsided and the wingman attributed it to an air strike. He tried to raise the crew of the case aircraft

at this time to see if it was his bombs but there was no answer. He attributed this to the aircraft being out of radio range. The aircraft was found to be missing when the wingman returned to his carrier. After the fact, the wingman estimated the fireball's location at the point that became the recorded location for the case. A search and rescue operation was initiated to that location and nothing found.

We had found this A-6 eighty kilometers south of where we had previously hunted for it. Our fluid style of investigation had again paid off with huge dividends for the families.

The next year JTF-FA sent an excavation team to that location. During the clearing of the vegetation on the crash site an identification tag was found which confirmed we had the right site. That aircrew was going home.

*   *   *

On that same series of mountains we were looking for another lost airplane crash site. The villagers knew of only one site but assumed it was a helicopter. We had a mandate to ensure it was not a site we were looking for and hatched a clever plan. The villagers did not think we could reach the site in one day because the rains had arrived on the mountain. It could be weeks before the weather cleared again. We decided to send villagers up to the crash site on an overnight trek. We gave a young male villager an instamatic camera, paper, and pen, in a waterproof bag. We asked him to get pictures of any major pieces of wreckage and write down any numbers they could find. Greg Parmele then used our helicopter to show them the type of numbers and wreckage we could use to correlate the aircraft.

While we completed the coordination of this plan, Sammy and Navy Lieutenant(jg) Castillo, an intelligence analyst, departed in the Squirrel to investigate another lead. They flew under the low cloud cover 15 kilometers to the northeast. There they stopped at a village right on the VN border. We knew a helicopter had crashed nearby but could not pinpoint the site. The villagers were very secretive and did not talk to outsiders. Therefore, for years the villagers would not acknowledge there were any crash sites nearby.

After the helicopter landed, 'fat Sammy' walked into the village trudging in mud up to his ankles. He walked to a hut and asked a sub-chief (same as an assistant) if there were any crash sites near the village. The man confirmed there was but could not say more. The chief was gone and we would have to come back. That was a huge coup as they had finally revealed the site was nearby.

Sammy and J.G. returned to our location brimming with excitement. We loaded both aircraft and went over to the village to see if we could locate the chief. We landed on opposite sides due to the size of the MI-17. As we slogged through the mud toward the chief's hut, we inspected piles of scrap metal. These piles were common in every village as they accumulate metal from the fields. Every so often the metals buyers would pass through and buy the village scrap piles. We immediately noticed scrap metal consistent with U.S. aircraft. Many pieces of a helicopter were under the pile. We inspected some of the larger pieces looking for data plates. There were none and we moved over to the chief's hut.

I had decided to stay out of the interviews because Sammy was already having good luck with the locals. When we got closer, Sammy informed us there were no people in the village. We would have to leave and try another day. This was a bad development but typical of what other teams had experienced in that particular village. We reloaded our helicopters and decided to call it a day. If we could finally crack this case it would be a major victory another of our missing heroes.

Circumstances of loss (Courtesy of POW/MIA Network):
On 9 June 1968, 37 miles west of Hue, a downed Marine Corps fighter pilot lay on the ground with a broken arm and leg. To his further misfortune he had parachuted into a North Vietnamese Army bivouac area. The enemy used him for bait to lure rescue helicopters within killing range. Air strikes pounded the site around the survivor. The first helicopter made three attempts to reach the Marine before breaking off to refuel. Lieutenant Rittichier dived his aircraft in for the pickup. Heavy fire, however, drove him away. He swung around to let the gunships sweep the terrain and then, followed them back into the area. As he hovered over the pilot, bullets punched his aircraft and set it afire. He tried to pull away, but his aircraft would not respond. The

helicopter settled to the ground and exploded. Within 30 seconds a ball of fire consumed the aircraft. Lieutenant Rittichier lost his life in nobly trying to save that of another. While the Air Force carries Rittichier on its rolls as "Missing in Action," the Coast Guard lists him as "Killed in Action, Body Not Recovered."

We came back to the village the next day and there were villagers conducting their daily business. We stayed at the helicopters as the local officials and Sammy talked to the chief. He agreed to show us the crash site and pointed to a grass field about a half-mile to the east. I went to the field straight away and awaited the arrival of the village chief.

Field of 10' tall grass on the VN/Laos border.

The chief was delayed and I became impatient. Therefore, I took the team into the field and started a line search. The grass was thick and well over our heads. We moved through the field skirting big bomb craters and reached the other end without finding anything. We then reversed our direction, went the other way, and still didn't find anything. Now I was even more impatient and irritated. I was becoming fearful that this opportunity could pass us by. The chief could easily decide not to "find" the crash site. Delay tactics were always a possibility in Laos.

The main rotor hub in a maze of grass.

The chief arrived and led us on a circuitous route through the middle of the field. At first he could not find what he was looking for and I thought my worst fears had come true again. After more searching, we heard a yell and moved through the grass toward the voice. There was the chief standing by the main rotor housing of a large helicopter. We searched the area and found signs of a burned aircraft. Melted metal remnants around the rotor hub provided evidence of extreme heat.

Bomb crater with burned boot remnants.

Sammy found pieces of a boot sole about ten feet away in a bomb crater. We focused our search in that area and numerous parts of boots and clothing were identified. This was the proof we needed to correlate this aircraft by location, type, and life support items. It was evidence that crewmembers were likely in the aircraft at the time of the incident. This was a very big find.

The crash site was located near a road paralleling the border. That made the site extremely susceptible to pillaging by Vietnamese metals and remains scavengers. Scavenging would violate the site and potentially remove the remains of the crewman before an excavation. I made a recommendation to the DET 3 Commander that we excavate this crash site at the first opportunity. The Commander was very receptive to the proposal because he needed an accessible site to excavate on the next JFA. The rainy season was setting in which required accessible sites.

Evidence the crew was likely onboard the burning aircraft.

A Recovery Element excavated the site and found twenty-two teeth. These teeth would provide the DNA evidence to positively identify the missing crewmembers. This would end our search for the last National Guard pilot missing from the war in Southeast Asia.

**Courtesy POW/MIA .Net
(http://www.faraway-soclose.org/jcr/)**

On 06 October, 2003, at 1300 hours, the remains of United States Coast Guard Lt. Jack Columbus Rittichier will be buried at Arlington National Cemetery. Jack was the first Coast Guardsman killed in action in Vietnam, and the only one who remained unaccounted for after the war's end. The crash site of the Jolly Green 23 was discovered on 09 November 02, and the remains of the four crew members were repatriated on 14 Feb 03.

*   *   *

During each JFA, the Investigation Element would work in a sequential order of provinces from south to north or north to south. As we departed each province, it was traditional to have a dinner or banquet with the local officials. We would jointly celebrate our successes and give mutual thanks for friendship and hospitality. Preparations for the banquet usually involved the American team purchasing a cow and/or a goat to be butchered and used to prepare the feast. The food was always meat, fish, and vegetables prepared in Lao traditional dishes.

I say usually because the Lao had some dietary customs that did not appeal to me. They revolved around the preparation of the goat. The goat would be purchased a few days in advance and tethered behind the hotel or base camp. It was fed a specific type of high quality forage and butchered the day of the event. His entire intestinal tract was removed intact and set off to the side—the feces still inside. The solid excrement would be squeezed out and discarded. The remainder, to include the non-solid feces, would be saved and used in their recipes. Sammy explained that Lao men liked a bitter taste on their palate. This was considered a special treat. I always told Sammy that I did not want to eat the 'shit soup.' He always sat beside me at the dinner table and promised to look after me.

In late 2002, we held a dinner as we prepared to leave Salavan Province. The room was full of big chuckles and whispers as the Lao waited to see if I would eat the hidden surprise. As soon as I entered the room I could smell it—shit soup. I sat at my chair with Sammy on my left. In the middle of the table was a big serving bowl on a platter. Inside the bowl was a steaming and smelly brew.

Typical Provincial farewell dinner.

Due to all the elbowing and chuckling on the Lao side, I decided I was going to eat the soup and act like it was no big deal. Sammy graciously filled my bowl. As I looked down at it in front of me I saw a foul brown broth with a few vegetable greens and small bits of meat. I took my spoon, and with everyone watching, I started to slurp my shit soup. Unfortunately, it tasted just like it smelled—like shit. Sammy quietly asked, "Do you know what you're eating?" He was not sure if I would get upset.

I answered under my breath, "Yeah, I know—I can smell it." The Lao at the table seemed very pleased with themselves and laughed at the fact I had actually ate the soup. It was a time for celebration and a round of Lao Lao was toasted by all. I spent the rest of the dinner wondering if I would get the "funk."

*   *   *

The Investigation Element was sent to reinvestigate a crash site in Khammouan Province, that had been located in the mid-1990's. The wreckage was widely dispersed across a four-hundred meter area. Prior to the investigation, I talked with Bill Gadoury, who had been the Team Leader at the time. He explained the crash site was dispersed over a large area and there was no definitive place to excavate.

We arrived at the site and scouted the wreckage pattern. It was spread across a thick grass covered hill top. The team broke into three parts. Sammy went with the witness to collect data on wreckage located by villagers in the area. Two search and survey teams would scout the edges of the wreckage field. This was where experience made a major impact. Each piece of wreckage, in a field such as this, would provide indicators of where the cockpit had gone. From the location of the landing struts and wheels, followed by the heavy wing flap retractors, we determined the orientation of the crash site. We followed the general direction of impact about four-hundred meters over the knoll, into a deep ravine. This was the final resting place of a very compressed aircraft engine. It had been severely damaged during impact. With this knowledge, and barring a late ejection by the crew, the pilot should be between point A and B.

We searched extensively, in the heat of the day, for about four hours. We found nothing to indicate a crewmember was in the aircraft at the time of impact. Then Reggie, Adam Pierce, and I found ourselves together in the ravine.

Reggie at the Lao Hi crock.

Reggie was looking for any serial numbers on the engine. Pierce and I were searching a thick area of scrub on a steep incline. I found a piece of canvas with snaps, belt, and a buckle. I then called Reggie over. He was exhausted from the heat and crawling around in the steep ravine. With sweat dripping from his brow, he glanced at my finds and said they were nothing of value. I disagreed and threw them in my rucksack anyway just to be sure.

Myself, Lao Official, and Sammy in Khammouan Province.

It would not be until we returned to Hawaii that Reggie would send me an email. The canvas was an F-4 Phantom seat cover. The belt and buckle were from a Martin Baker Ejection Seat. I was ecstatic and went directly to Reggies' office to give him a hard time. On my first crash site survey I would have never known the significance of that wreckage. After surveying numerous crash sites, across Laos and Cambodia, I had become a very effective Team Leader.

*   *   *

On this trip, we had one of the best teams we had in two years. We also had the pleasure of training Sergeant Brown (USMC) on his first trip into Laos. He was a slender guy with a passion for cigarettes and Pepsi. He was attempting to get a grasp for our operations. He became a bit defensive and irritated as too many suggestions were being thrown his direction. Nothing he did seemed to be right and everything became funny. On one day, we went to a village to investigate the possibility of a crash site in the area. The old village chief insisted we come to his hootch. He wanted to have an official interview in his house.

The old guy thought this was a special day and out came the "Lao Lao" to toast the occasion. This particular brew was extremely harsh and brought tears to my eyes. It burned my lips, and the inside of my mouth and throat, making them tingle and go numb. In typical fashion the Lao toasted with half-shots of Lao Lao while the American guests got the full treatment. Brown made it clear to the team that he had no intention of drinking any of the Lao Lao. I explained at length that as the lead analyst he would be asking questions to the witnesses. It would be proper protocol to at least have a small toast with the chief. The chief then presented each guest a full glass of alcohol. Brown wanted to refuse it but the circumstances did not present a way to refuse the toast. After a ceremonial toast, the entire group gulped down a shot. Brown was in pain but happy it was over.

What he did not realize was a single shot glass would continue around the room until the entire bottle was drained. When he noticed it coming his way again his eyes got big and he whispered, "I'm not gonna have any more." Death looks shot his way from every other American because that meant we would have to drink his share also. He got the hint and down went another shot. His face got red and his eyes watered.

Lao village in Savannakhet Province.

MSG Collins said, "Time to call in the B-team." With that he got on the radio and called the other half of the team waiting in the MI-17, telling them to report to the chiefs' hut. The plan was to call in the B-team, and spread the wealth of the alcohol so no one had to have too much. In they came and joined the circle. The bottle was drained and all was good.

The chief, seeing his bottle was empty, jabbered something to his wife. Soon a young Lao man appeared with a half-full bottle of clear liquid. This was obviously the chief's special private stock. Around it came again and Brown whispered, "If I have another, I'm going to puke." Again came the death looks and again he took it for the team. He didn't puke, but he was "gone." Three shots and he was left staring out the window. The chief was happy and the interview began.

Toasting with the village chief.

I noticed Brown wasn't taking notes so I poked him and asked if he got the information. "What? Oh!" and he tried to concentrate. The linguist said, "The chief is 78 years old." And Brown looked back with a pained look on his face and squeaked, "The chief is 78 years old?"

"Yeah, dude. Write it down!" That was how the whole interview went. Brown had mush for a brain and we left him to watch the open window as we conducted the interview for him.

*   *   *

In early 2003, we returned to investigate the same case that had inspired Earl Swift's book. Many teams had investigated the case, and none had come to the correct correlation. This included my erroneous determination. Our work to crack this one had begun back in Hawaii. We spent long hours of pouring over the maps and reading previous investigation reports and historical records. We formed a plan to start atop the plateau. I wanted to get a feel for the battlefield and the events of the fateful day our aircraft was lost.

It was a wide-open expanse of rolling five-foot grass and reminded me of the "Little Bighorn Battlefield." On the hilltop, were three crash sites that were accounted for in the historical records. We split the team into sections and visited each one. Each of the sites had considerable evidence which even included a body armor breastplate. None of these could be the case aircraft. The case aircraft had completed a pick-up and departed the plateau before going down.

Yan Collins and I stood, surveyed the terrain, and discussed fields of fire. We speculated how we would have approached the area as a helicopter pilot attempting to complete an extraction. We took a lot of time to re-walk the plateau top battlefield and speculate on the flight pattern of our missing bird. Based on what we already knew of the crash sites on the ground below the plateau, we determined a likely egress (departure) route as heading northeast off the summit.

We flew down to the road below, in the Squirrel and MI-17, and began to walk the road that crossed over district borders. I had seen this problem coming because a district line went right through the area in question. Therefore, we had officials present from both districts.

We planned to stop at every village along the way. At the second set of huts, we encountered a village not on the maps. If three huts could be a village, this was a village. It was an unnamed village, and no one had ever found this site. Two minutes later, the villagers said they had a crash site within their village area on the mountain. The villagers indicated the crash site was up against the vertical cliff of the mountain and surrounds by huge boulders. I was extremely happy at this point. This was a tough case to crack and it looked like we could make amends for the wasted excavation. We hired the villagers to clear the site so we could land as close as possible the next day.

On our return, we spotted the cleared area and landed in a nearby rice field. We then moved by foot to the site the villagers had also cleared. There was not much metal because of the scavenging by the villagers. We did locate cloth, flight suit material, earmuffs, communications headpieces, and helmet parts. Then Master Sergeant Collins found a tooth with a restoration in it. We finally had what we were after. We had found physical remains, which made this site a priority to excavate. We broke out the satellite phone and called Bill Forsythe in Hawaii. I said, "Bill, you won't believe where we are standing right now!" Bill was extremely pleased. He felt this helicopter crew was composed of heroes who sacrificed everything that day. By finding physical remains, we could bring them home that much sooner. We recommended it for excavation and were very pleased we had made good after my earlier erroneous recommendation.

After we arrive back in Hawaii, Earl Swift called and asked how we felt when we found the site. I told him we were pleased but that we had also just found a site earlier in the day. I explained we were just taking care of business for the families. I then asked Earl when he would publish the rest of the story on the final success of the case. He promised it would be forthcoming.

Trekking the mountains in the mud and rain.

*   *   *

Chapter 7
Isolated Burials

The investigation of American civilian Eugene Debruin was an interesting challenge. "Chief," Sammy, and I played a major role in bringing some resolution to at least a portion of this case.

Eugene Debruin was an Air America door kicker on a C-47 transport plane. His aircraft crashed in Phin District, Savannakhet Province, Laos, in 1963. They were transporting cattle and were hit by ground fire. It was reported two members of the crew died in the crash. Mr. Debruin and four non-Americans parachuted from the crash and were captured. They were held by the Pathet Lao through 1965. Also held in that camp were Navy Lt. Dieter Dengler and 1LT Duane Martine.

On February 1, 1966, U.S. Navy Lt. Dieter Dengler departed the aircraft carrier USS RANGER in an A1H Sky raider. He was shot down and captured. First Lt. Duane W. Martin was an HH-3 helicopter pilot who was captured after his aircraft went down in Vietnam.

On June 29, 1965, this group of prisoners made an escape attempt. In the escape, four of seven Lao guards were killed. What happened next became a confused story as to who was traveling with whom. It was thought Eugene Debruin was recaptured. Deiter Dengler reported he and First Lt. Duane W. Martin had traveled together. What happened next has been the subject of great debate in POW/MIA circles.

We interviewed at a village in Khammouan Province. At this village, two key witnesses were reported to have firsthand knowledge of an incident involving two American POWs. The POWs had attempted to obtain food from their village and were discovered by the villagers. One POW was killed by a villager with a machete. The other fled the area and was eventually rescued. This story had previously been correlated to Dieter Dengler and Duane Martin. Dieter Dengler was rescued after twenty-two days on the run. During his debriefing he said he witnessed Duane Martin killed by a machete-wielding villager. The information was credible enough that JTF-FA conducted an excavation in the area identified—no evidence was found.

Both witnesses were elderly thin Lao men. One was quite tall at about six feet and one shorter at about five foot nine. The taller man took us on a walk of the area two times. He claimed an American had been buried in a hole the village had used during the war to get away from bombings. He said the hole was quite deep and he couldn't see over the edge if standing inside. He told Sammy when the officials were not listening, "You know, I'm old and I can't remember." He pointed at the shorter man and said, "He knows." He explained that the shorter witness had killed the American with a machete and kept the tooth.

We began to intensively question the shorter witness. The shorter man always wore his Lao Army shirt. You could tell by looking at his eyes that he was mentally sharp. He claimed to have once had a dental bridge from the prisoner but had lost it. He told us he had thrown it in the woods inside a ball of rice. He felt this offering would appease evil spirits that brought bad luck. We searched that area using a metal detector with no result. All indications were this man still had the tooth.

On our second visit to the village, "Chief" and I were told to stay by the aircraft as Lao officials talked to the man. They returned and said the man now had the tooth but would not give it up. I replied that we needed to obtain the tooth as evidence. The official then asked me how much we were willing to pay for it. I hesitated and asked what he meant. The official explained that the old man had previously been offered fifty workers worth of compensation for the tooth by a previous Team Leader. I did the quick math in my head, which meant a previous Team Leader had offered $1,250 for that tooth. There was no telling how much of that money would actually make it to the man with the tooth. This was a society where graft was culturally expected. It was likely that each level of officials, to include the village chief, would also get a cut of the money.

This was a sticky situation as a precedent had already been established. I looked at "Chief" standing next to me and he just shrugged his shoulders. I considered the fact that a considerable amount of money, time, and effort, had been expended on this case. This included two excavations based on this proven liar's word. I then told the official I did not want to pay anything. He replied that if I did not pay—we would never get the tooth. I then told him I would pay 40 workers. My rationale was maybe we would haggle and I wanted to see the tooth that no westerner had ever seen. I reasoned that once he revealed the tooth he would likely lose his bargaining power. Then it would become an official issue to acquire that tooth and return it to the Debruin family. My offer was rejected outright and we departed the village again without seeing the evidence.

That dental bridge had become the witness's biggest treasure in life. It had gotten him celebrity status since the Americans would come to visit him periodically. Two excavations based on his lies had employed the entire village. He knew there would be a big payoff.

Months later, on another JFA, we sat in a circle on the old man's porch and the Lao officials began to lose their patience. They aggressively questioned the old man with the tooth and his twenty-year-old son. I was actually amazed. Even "Chief" was surprised at this aggressive tactic. The man's son got nervous and called him aside to talk. In the end the man, with confidence in his eyes, retorted, "I am old. What are you going to do? Cut my head off?"

We returned to the village a few months later to make another attempt to recover the dental bridge. It was rumored that during the period between our visits the old man's son was put in jail. Their village was then informed he would not be released until the old man agreed to give up the tooth.

We arrived at the village, sat again in a small circle around the village chief's porch. The man pulled an old glass cold cream container with a screw top lid from the upper left breast pocket of his shirt. Carefully, he opened the glass container, reached inside with two fingers, and held up his pride and joy. I felt a sense of satisfaction and frustration based irritation. We had waited years for this moment—the Debuin family had been kept waiting for years. I sent the Squirrel back to Ban Alang Base Camp to get Gwen Haugen, the anthropologist, to come back to the village and inspect the tooth.

Gwen was the anthropologist who had headed up the excavation to find this tooth or the main remains. When she arrived, she joined the circle and inspected the bridge. In the interim, I had sketched and measured the tooth. Gwen inspected it and determined it was consistent with dental records from Eugene Debruin. She held up the tooth to the man and in an irritated tone said, "Do you know how much time and effort I put into finding this tooth?" The man just had a big smile on his face as he enjoyed the moment. At this point, we were not allowed to photograph it or take it with us. The Lao Team national officials assured us they would procure the dental bridge in consultation with district officials.

The tooth found its way to JTF-FA custody via the Lao Team and was taken to CILHI. Only time will tell whether this would be the end of the story. After all, a restoration could be separated from the man. I heard later on that every hut in that village received new tin on their roofs in exchange for the tooth. The shifty witness would always be a local hero.

*　　*　　*

Any compensation for remains or evidence was always a touchy issue. After the Detachment 3 Commander changed, the new commander LTC Kevin Smith came to Hawaii with a Lao delegation for consultative talks. During the visit, I sat with LTC Smith and Gunny Carabello in LTC Smiths' room in the Hilton Hawaiian Village. I specifically asked LTC Smith what his guidance was for the future in Laos in those situations. He was irritated I had not received clear guidance in the past and came to a decision. This was important because whatever I did would affect his negotiations and coordination during his tenure.

LTC Smith told me that if the situation were ever to occur, he wanted to have a maximum of twenty-five workers offered and the work for which they were hired had better occur. For example, buy an LZ and actually get an LZ. It was my job to monitor, and although there seemed to be a gray line, I was to stay legal. Finally, I had some guidance.

This issue immediately came to a head in the recovery of the brother of the former Governor of Vermont and current head of the Democratic National Committee, Howard Dean. The search for Charles Dean and Neal Sharman is a long story that started on my first JFA as Team Leader. It ended after I had left JTF-FA.

*　　*　　*

In 1974, Charles Dean and Neal Sharman were traveling down the Mekong River on a boat from Vientiane to an area around Pakse. Their boat was intercepted by Pathet Lao troops and they were taken captive for being foreigners with cameras. Their movement was tracked to a village eight miles from the Vietnam Border, in Khammouan province. They were held in the village jail for a short period of time. The story has it that the U.S. and Australian governments protested their detention. Neil Sharman was offered the opportunity to leave. He refused and chose to stay with Charles Dean. What happened to them after that point became a mystery.

In 1998, a team interviewed a Lao official that later led them to a field adjacent to the road heading into Vietnam. This field was also about one mile from the border. He identified an area near the road and the team recommended an excavation.

In 2001, "Chief," Sammy, and I entered a village about four miles south from the field. We began an interview of the village elders to try and locate any other first hand witnesses to the fate of Mr. Sharman and Mr. Dean. An older man, perhaps in his late 60s approached and said he knew what happened to them. He said he had been responsible for security of the road from their village to the Vietnam border. One morning during the war he traveled the road and noticed something out of place in the field. He then stopped to investigate.

At the time, there was a camp for soldiers working on the road. The camp was surrounded with fighting positions. He noticed a foxhole had a cover on it and flipped it open. Inside were the bodies of Mr. Dean and Mr. Sharman. He gave a very graphic story about his supposition of the events that had occurred. He supposed they had been taken to the border where the VN guards had turned them back. At that point, the Lao captors had to decide what to do with their prisoners. Instead of choosing to release them, they chose to end their lives. They made them get into the foxhole, one on top of the other. Then shot them as they held up their hands to shield themselves. The detail with which he explained the events suggested he may have been present at the time of the executions.

We asked why he was so confident he could find the location of the grave. He reached in his left pocket and pulled out a piece of bone holding it up for us to see. With confidence he said he had cut it off the shin bone of "the one on top." He said he had gotten sick and a Shaman told him he needed to get a piece of bone to use as a medicinal charm. Americans were big so they had big medicine. He handed it to us. I turned it over and over and studied it closely. I had seen many animal bones and this did not look like an animal bone. I was not an expert but it looked like it could have come from a shin bone.

As Chief continued to question the witness, I leaned behind him and told the official we would need to get that bone. I estimated there could be enough bone to test for DNA since it was about one inch wide and two inches long. I wasn't sure, but the anthropologists were at the base camp in the next province to the south. I sketched the edges of the bone to have a relative size to show the anthropologists in the event we couldn't procure the bone.

After the questioning was completed, I again asked the official to ask for the bone. He said we would discuss it later in the evening back at our base camp. I was not happy, but there was money to be had and the precedent had been set. We returned the bone to the witness who put it in his pocket. We made an appointment to have him accompany us to the burial site the next day.

That evening the Lao official asked what I was willing to give for the bone. I fell back on my guidance and said I would give twenty-five workers of compensation, but I wanted a landing zone cut at the site. Sammy informed me that the officials were upset with my low offer of compensation. They further explained that we had destroyed their country during the war and compensation was justified. This was another snapshot into the mentality of compensation now for acts of war of thirty years prior. Time in the Asian culture was immaterial.

We interviewed that same old witness and a half-dozen more over the next two years. Each took us to the field to show us where he thought the grave would be. They were all generally within eighty meters of each—eighty meters was a huge area to excavate. This was not the area recommended by the 1999 team, but much farther from the road. There was a lot of general knowledge of the correct field but we lacked that definitive spot to excavate.

"Chief" and I talked often about how to excavate that site. The problem was compounded by the fact that the field had been graded during construction of the road. Farmers made a series of irrigated rice fields (little ponds) across the whole thing, except for one small square about 10 by 10 feet. I had "Chief" ask the farmer why he hadn't farmed that spot. The farmer replied that he didn't have time. These people were seriously superstitious and huge opportunists. We talked often about the possibility that patch was the grave site.

In the end, we recommended a larger area and also recommended a road grader be brought in. The whole area would be done a layer at a time. In the first couple days, the excavation team hit the grave and retrieved the remains of Neil Sharman and Richard Dean. Richard Dean was the brother of the Governor of Vermont, Howard Dean. Mr. Sharman and Mr. Dean were going home.

I had the opportunity to see an aerial photo of the excavation and location of the gravesite in relation to the field. It looked to be just to the south of where the unused square of soil was located.

*   *   *

In 2002, we had ended our stay at the forestry camp outside of Xepon, Savannakhet Province. To say thank you for the hospitality during our stay, we again had a dinner with the Lao officials. As usual we paid for the cow and beer and the officials provided the Lao Lao and Lao Hi. The cow and a goat would be butchered that day. Local foods would be prepared by the cooks who were contracted to feed the Lao officials.

After the usual toasts and formalities we stayed to drink beer and toast some more. The Lao officials then announced it was time to bestow each team member with their appropriate Lao names. We had spent years working together we had earned the privilege of this honor. This ceremony was conducted with dramatic fanfare and a level of respect and camaraderie. When it was my turn, the officials deliberated for a short while, broke their small huddle, and with great animation began their entertaining delivery of my name. They said that over the past years they had watched me work. They considered me very smart and very lucky. This was proven by solving many tough and famous cases. They thought it was funny how I used to chide the officials each day as we loaded the aircraft. I used to say, "This is going to be a lucky day!" They would just laugh. Later that day they would say, "You are a very lucky man!" after we had more success in our investigations. Therefore, my name would be "Bouna" (boo nah); the English translation ... "Thick Luck."

Chapter 8
The Killing Fields

During my second two years at JTF-FA, it was decided I would also assume the duties as the Cambodian Team Leader. This was an unexpected opportunity to investigate sites in another exotic country.

Operations in Cambodia were controlled from Phnom Phen, which served as a hub for personnel and equipment. The political climate in Cambodia was very different from Laos and Vietnam. The Cambodians were eager for more investigations and activity in their country. They recognized the monetary benefits and promoted internal investigation of cases. There had been a more limited number of losses in Cambodia mostly concentrated along the Cambodia/Vietnam border area. During the war, the U.S. inserted reconnaissance teams into this area to gain intelligence on Vietnamese troop movements. The Vietnamese had drifted deep into Cambodia to avoid the bombing of the Ho Chi Min trail. American aircraft had been lost deep inside Cambodia as they had transited from Thailand and South Vietnam for bombing, recon and logistics missions.

A large number of the losses inside Cambodia actually involved American journalists missing after the Khmer Rouge came to power in the mid-1970s. During this purge of the Cambodian people, numerous journalists tried to flee from Phnom Penh to Sihanoukville along the southern coast. It was their intent to try to reach the coast and get transportation away from the killing fields of Cambodia.

On my first mission to Cambodia I was asked to investigate a case involving the potential loss of numerous reporters in central Cambodia. A journalist named Zailin Grant had been conducting his own investigation into the loss of his friend

Dana Flynn. He speculated that Flynn had been held with other reporters near Kratie for a period of time and then executed in a nearby buffalo wallow.

The team and I reached the hotel in Kratie and met with Zailin Grant on the lanai (tropical porch). We immediately sat down with him as he explained his investigation and conclusion that the journalists were buried nearby. It was not my intent to rely unilaterally on the evidence Zailin had gathered during his investigation. We intended to compare his evidence to our records and come to a conclusion based on fact. My team had used its expertise to achieve great results in Laos and I intended to use our experience in Cambodia. We had done our homework and were determined to come to the best conclusion possible for this case.

Mr. Grant appeared to take offense when I said our team would start the investigation from scratch. In my view, it was necessary to revisit and validate any existing evidence and hopefully generate additional evidence and leads. If the evidence supported Zailins' conclusions, then we would all be successful in bringing another American home. If the evidence did not support his conclusions, then we needed to expand our base of investigation and be prepared for an alternate conclusion. Additionally, our team and JTF-FA did not have a mono-focus. We investigated all cases in the hope of generating leads to other potential losses in the area and in general.

Zailin also seemed to take offense to our demeanor, military style of dress, and interview techniques. This was our Lao core team. We were physically strong, very focused on our business, and experienced. Our technique was proven and we knew how to be culturally sensitive.

Zailin requested one additional day to complete his interviews and then he would step out of our way. This situation became awkward as he was in the general area of where we needed to work. I wanted to be a team player but I also needed to be able to interview the same folks he had just interviewed. There was no way to gauge the information the witnesses actually knew on their own or what they had just been introduced to by Zailin and his translator, Sos Kem. Our interpretation of the interview results would be based on the team's experience and analysis. If there were a disparity to Zailins' conclusions, that was okay. We just needed to keep gathering information from which to make a recommendation. Zailin had focused on one set of buffalo wallows. He surmised the reporters had been held as a group in an old Japanese camp on the outskirts of the town and then executed in those wallows.

One night at dinner time, Greg Parmele suggested we go down to a diner Zailin usually ate at to see how he had done that day in his investigation. We were trying to succeed in this investigation and keep Zailin abreast of our progress. We arrived at the diner, said hello, and then sat together at the table for dinner. We started to talk about the day and the conversation drifted to the overall POW/MIA effort in general.

Zailin made it plain that he was dissatisfied with the progress of investigations in Cambodia. He felt we should put a team of single men there year round to do continuous investigations. Tom Monroe was our intelligence analyst and very knowledgeable with investigation initiatives in Cambodia. Tom explained the pace of investigations in Cambodia was proportional to the remaining cases in Laos, Cambodia, and Vietnam.

Zailin was an Army Military Intelligence Officer in the Vietnam War and very passionate in his efforts to find his lost friends. I assumed we had an internal and common bond. At the same time, I felt he insulted my team member's work ethic and seemed to be baiting us with his questions. We talked strongly—as men do.

During the conversation between Zailin, Tom Monroe, and Joe Fraley, I listened for a period of time but did not join in. To join in was not my style. I always sat and listened and analyzed the information coming out. There was no point in debating the efforts of my organization in Cambodia.

I had actually started drinking some Cambodian beers and chatted with Dana Stone. Dana was an American reporter who was accompanying Zailin. By this time, I was distracted by all the chatter around me and said I wanted to get out of the line of fire. I meant get out of the line of noise of the other conversation so I could finish talking about beer with Dana. Zailin tells a different version. I encourage any reader of this book to look up his version on the internet. http://www.pythiapress.com/letters/war3.htm

*   *   *

We dug a long trench by hand in the buffalo wallow that Zailin thought had the highest probability of success. The task was very difficult in the sun baked soil and it required spuds (heavy metal poles) to break the crust. To complicate matters, the weather was extremely hot and the sun baked us as well as the soil. I helped the Cambodian work crew by getting in the trench and digging away. It was hot, but the team was in shape. It was too hot for Zailin and he departed to cool down. We worked through the day and sifted every bit of moved dirt and found nothing. In reality, it would have been a miracle to have found something there. Even in cases where a person knows he buried someone the location of the site can be off a couple of feet either direction.

We found nothing in the trench, interviewed the same witnesses that Zailin had identified, and also interviewed elders at every village surrounding the site. No evidence surfaced to support the buffalo wallow theory. There were reports of Caucasian military men held in the area during the war but nothing tangible to pursue.

The digging of the trench had completed our investigation on that case for this trip. I sat in the hotel and talked with Zailin before he departed for Phnom Penh and we moved on to another investigation. I sincerely told him it was a pleasure and I was sorry we hadn't been successful. I liked Zailin and knew exactly what it felt like not to be successful. For our team, it happened on every trip to Southeast Asia; but success was only the next trip away. As always, the POW/MIA issue was very controversial and emotional; I shook hands with Zailin and we parted ways. He left for Phnom Penh, and we began the investigation of a number of other cases across eastern Cambodia.

We would not know it at the time, but Zailin would send a letter with his observations of the investigation and his opinions to Ann Mills Griffith at the American League of Families. This in turn was handed over to General Redmann, Commander of Joint Task Force Full Accounting. It made its way to Colonel Neil Fox, the Deputy Commander. I was summoned to Colonel Fox's office and provided the opportunity to see Zailin's report. It was very unflattering and questioned our work in Cambodia. I was very disappointed that our efforts during this investigation would be reported in such a negative light. Our team was not in Cambodia to further anyone's personal agenda—we were there to recover missing Americans.

*   *   *

In Cambodia, we primarily revisited sites that had already been investigated or excavated. I knew Joe Patterson, the previous Cambodian Team Leader, had done great work before us and it was evident. We recommended numerous sites for re-excavation due to the hasty methods that had been used during the 1990's. In addition, we recommended a handful of isolated burial sites based on firsthand witness testimony.

During investigations in Kratie Province our team was tasked to resurvey a known Huey crash site thirty minutes to the southeast. This was the location of a battle between South Vietnamese and North Vietnamese forces. At least two helicopters were also lost within 500 meters of the battlefield. The fate of the crews became confused as they became separated and attempted to evade enemy troops.

The Huey site had been found but a previous excavation had failed to produce any evidence of remains. We re-investigated the site and conducted another survey, which would set the stage for another excavation. The helicopter had landed in a thickly forested area alongside a small stream. It impacted a large tree and then strewn wreckage across a twenty meter radius on a gradual slope. Our survey served to expand the excavation of the previous team and slightly uphill. We did our job and then departed.

During our investigation with Zailin Grant a Recovery Element had begun excavation of the Huey site. They continued the excavation during our stay at Kratie but failed to find evidence of remains. The Anthropologist then determined the excavation was complete. As the Recovery Element prepared the site for final photos, they scraped the edges of the excavated site to make crisp edges. As a worker scraped, a tooth rolled out of the edge of the curb. The team then expanded the excavation a few more meters uphill and found success. They found the shallow grave of a crew member from the helicopter. The remains were intact and the crewman still wore his helmet and uniform.

We were informed of the discovery at the hotel and took the opportunity to visit the site the next day. When we arrived, it was an incredibly gratifying scene. The excavation team was painstakingly removing soil from the remains using small brushes and spoons. The remains laid in the grave in almost pristine condition. The skull was still in the helmet and the skeleton still wore a flight suit in exceptionally good condition. This undisturbed condition would facilitate a complete recovery of the remains. This was the result of a team effort and the most complete and undisturbed set of remains and personal effects that I would witness during my time at JTF-FA.

*   *   *

The Vietnamese were also conducting a national effort to recover their war dead from Cambodia. The difference was they only recovered North Vietnamese soldier's remains from the war. They had no interest in recovering the South Vietnamese soldiers. Since we had reports of U.S. POWs buried in the Vietnamese graveyards, we visited reported areas of Vietnamese hospitals in remote areas of northeastern Cambodia.

As we walked through the jungle, I almost failed to notice we were in a graveyard. We were in an area covered with dense canopy. The floor of the jungle had sparse ferns and leafy plants growing in a white sandy soil. I noticed a rock about six inches around sitting on top of the sand. I looked further and found another and then another. The rocks were in straight lines amongst the vegetation. Each of these rocks marked an individual gravesite. The underside of each rock had an etched number corresponding to the grave. Under the rock was a glass vial, inside which was a piece of paper identifying the soldier in the grave. It was very orderly.

This did not help our problem of finding possible POWs in the vicinity of these graveyards. There were numerous stories and rumors of possible gravesites and sightings of POWs. These stories circumstantially correlated to actual known losses. Sometimes I felt it was like reading a horoscope. If you tell enough stories, they are bound to correlate to something. The problem was you had to give each story the maximum legitimate attention because it could lead to finding one of our fallen comrades.

*   *   *

During our interviews in the area of Kratie, we heard terrible stories of the methods used by the Khmer Rouge to kill anyone they deemed a threat to their regime. They had rounded up local people and put them in an internment camp on the outer city limits of Kratie. We interviewed one survivor of the camp, an old farmer who had been held for a period of weeks and then released. He said in the middle of the night they would come into the sleeping area and escort certain individuals out behind the compound to the edge of a pond. There they would tell the people to be quiet and not make a fuss or they would later kill their entire family. Then to keep things quiet they would hit the person over the head with a club or hammer and kill them. He told stories of people who had been hit but not killed who screamed and tried to run before they were finished off.

He said the Khmer Rouge were short of ammunition and had developed a ploy where they would have the person get on their knees and then take a string and tie a loop on each end and slip it over the thumbs of the victim. They then told the person that if they made noise or broke the string that they would kill all of their family. The person would then have to sit still and wait his turn as other people were killed first. His stories were very graphic and credible since this was a documented killing field of the Khmer Rouge.

We followed the trail of another missing journalist on the information of an accountant in Phnom Penh whose entire family had been killed. There was an island in the middle of the Mekong River that people would be taken to and then executed. This provided security from the area villages as they would not know what had happened to those taken into custody. In this case the trail of the journalist was specific and we talked to people who had seen him, knew his name, and had actually shot pigeons for him to eat. Then one day he was taken to the village chief's for a day out. He had dinner at the hut, played with the chief's children, and then was taken by boat to the island and executed. The locals claimed the entire island moved almost annually with the flow of the Mekong River. Recovery of anyone from that island could prove impossible.

In Cambodia our vocation is very difficult because the Khmer Rouge had conducted a social purging which was where the term of Killing Fields came from. Educated people from the cities were sent to the rice fields and killed. This social purging along with losses due to the war had left a generational void. Also gone were the possible witnesses we needed to find our missing servicemen and citizens (journalists).

The purging of the Khmer Rouge continued until the Vietnamese removed them in 1979. You have to visit Cambodia to realize the vast social criminality of what happened there. Our journalists got caught in the fray and it will be extremely difficult to find the clues to bring them home. To visit these places where you know countless people were tortured and executed left you with an unsettled feeling. Don Guthrie, one of our Kiwi pilots, said it best when he described his visit to the Killing Field. In his Queens' English drawl he whispered, "C'mon, let's get out of 'ere, it's givin' me the "willies."

*   *   *

I put together a set of principles I had learned the hard way over the first two years and gave them to the team as a way to focus before each mission. They shed much light on the techniques we used very successfully in Laos. Many families wondered what the hell we were doing there and how we came to any conclusions at all. These tenants paid off.

Lao witness describes a crash site in his village area.

Lost aircraft were likely located within an eight kilometer radius of the record loss location. This was determined from experience during our investigations. The record loss locations were usually generated by a witness to the incident. Navigation in an aircraft in flight, or from a soldier on foot in the jungle, was very difficult. Therefore, one must allow a margin for error.

It was important to make a comparison of the record loss location, Search and Rescue (SAR) loss location, record 559 (radar tracking) document and look for any consistencies as they plotted on the map. If those three data bases were consistent, then the crash site was likely nearby. You just needed to visited the correct village or find the right witness.

Any site surveys prior to 1998 should be considered as questionable. Early investigations in Laos were done quickly as teams had too many cases to investigate in thirty days. It caused a frantic pace and resulted in marginal work.

Include the Lao officials and they will help you. They are not the enemy to deceive. Success is based on the help of the district officials. They can speak the local dialects and convince the witnesses they have nothing to be afraid of by telling the truth.

Make it plain you are only interested in finding the remains and have no interest in metal or taking anything else away. Also, you don't care who scavenged the metal. You just want the remains.

Ground searches based on aerial imagery are a waste of time and effort. The only exception is a photo with a very specific and prominent feature.

Ground searches based on reporting from war era searches are bogus. Always find a local to lead you to a site.

If a site is remote, hire local villagers to cut an LZ for use on another day. Also, have them clear the crash site for you to make searching it easier. Maximize time.

If weather or the schedule is a problem, take instamatic cameras with you and give one to the team you send to the crash sites. If weather goes to heck, you can at least get the camera back and see what was there.

Always ask witnesses if another American team has been there prior and what they did. Just because they have been to the village doesn't mean they found out about all the crash sites.

You have to ask the witnesses about *every detail,* or they won't tell you.

If you ask village elders if they know about any other crash sites and they say, "No," ask about crash sites they have heard of in other village areas. They won't say unless you specifically ask. Then they might not actually say but tell you to go to a village and ask *them* about it.

Remote or difficult sites allegedly visited by a prior team equal missing aircraft. Teams before 2000 always worked too quickly and missed some easy finds.

Never pay for a bone, media item or personal effect. It is Pandora's Box and will come back to haunt you.

During case packet preparation, make sure you have all the Detailed Reports of Investigation from previous investigations. Read them. Also, look at Bright light (POW/MIA data base) and become familiar with the other cases that are located in the area of the case you are investigating. Many times you will find something you hadn't even counted on.

If you get information on a crash and think you may have trouble getting to it, chances are all previous teams thought the same thing. It will be a good find when you get there.

*   *   *

On September 11, 2001, I was walking into the front lobby of our hotel in Pattaya, Thailand. Just inside the entrance was a small bar with a television turned on. I noticed someone I needed to talk to having a beer and walked over. I glanced up and saw live footage talking about an airplane having hit the World Trade Center. Then I watched live as the second airplane hit the other tower. We continued to watch as the first tower fell down. Someone asked, "Was that real?" We watched the events unfold in silence. Another unknown voice said, "Someone is gonna pay!"

We had to wait in Thailand for days for a ride home because our aircraft had been diverted to other missions. We waited wondering like everyone one else what the impact would be in the near future. 9/11 would coincide with decisions I had to make within my personal military career.

I stood on the bank of the Mekong River, on the Cambodia/Laos border, and talked to my Army personnel manager. He asked me where I wanted to be stationed and I said I'd like to stay in Hawaii. He said to consider it done and five months later I would shift to the 25th Infantry Division (Light), Schofield Barracks, Hawaii. The 25th ID was rumored to be in the hopper for deployment and it was a perfect fit for me in the last few years of my career. The Executive Officer of the Division Artillery had promised to send me as an individual augmenter to Afghanistan early in the summer. I was anxious to have my chance to deploy to the desert and contribute to the War on Terrorism. My time at Joint Task Force Full Accounting was almost at an end. I knew there would never be another job like this one. This was a noble opportunity to bring home the missing and directly impact the live of many families. I hated the realization of the finality of my time in the POW/MIA effort upon my departure.

*   *   *

Air Assault School

In December 2002, I attended the Army Air Assault School at Schofield Barracks, Hawaii. One of our team members had attended the school in September and failed the first day hazing period. To his credit he made the effort to attend the school. Not to his credit, he was home the same day. I had been encouraging my entire team to attend the school but no one would take the challenge. After one team member came back unsuccessful, I decided to attend the class myself and set the example for my team. I also wanted the team to know that the Air Assault School was nothing to be feared. It was a great opportunity.

In the second week of December, I gathered with around two hundred other soldiers in an open field on Schofield Barracks. It was early in the morning and very dark. I had my prescribed packing list for the course in a waterproof bag at my feet and stood in formation. "Black Hats" (instructors) from the Air Assault Cadre began calling names of the primary candidates and then moved to the alternate list. Not all the soldiers would get in the class but MSGT Collins came over from Camp Smith to ensure I would get one of the slots. It was no big issue and I was in.

We loaded the back of eight trucks and drove thirty minutes through the darkness to a parking lot in the middle of the woods. We quickly downloaded and moved into formation. The long awaited dogging period began. On our face in the wet mud of the dirt road we did push-ups, sit-ups, mountain climbers, roll left and roll right. In the first ten minutes, we were official mud puppies. We then charged into the pit (a sawdust physical fitness area) and began an hour long period of exercises. All along the edges cadre would walk the pit, dare you to quit and make sure you were not sloughing.

I found it interesting to be in the pit—actually, almost nostalgic. I hadn't been in this environment for years. This was the first time since I had become an officer. Everyone was trying hard and I was actually pleased to see no one was quitting. This was also the first school I had attended since Airborne School that included female soldiers. They too seemed to be doing fine and were just as determined to succeed.

About a half hour into the dogging, we were doing a period of standing with our arms extended straight out to the sides without letting them drop. We continually did small arm circles to the rear and then small circles to the front. It was then I realized the folly of lifting heavy weights in the gym until two days before the school. I couldn't keep my arms straight out because my shoulders wouldn't function. I tried to extend my arms back out but they wouldn't go. Next thing I knew had a black hat dogging me for being weak.

It had been a long time since I had been in a school environment but I truly enjoyed the opportunity to be a soldier again. We began a five day period of classroom instruction focused on aircraft types and Pathfinder operations very similar to what I had done in Pathfinder School. Each morning was filled with PT, runs that gradually increased in length, and four road marches. The road marches were of increasing lengths and speeds. They prepared the class for the final and required twelve-mile road march.

I noticed right away during physical training that even at forty-one years old, I was stronger, both mentally and physically, than the majority of the younger soldiers. As I expected, my experience was far ahead of the remainder of the class.

We took a series of three book tests after which I was number one in the class. I was familiar with the air assault operations and spent the time at night to study the material. I wanted to prove to myself I was still competitive and the diligent study paid off.

The sling load inspections were identical to Pathfinder School and I did well, but the big event was the rappelling training. I found it exceptional, and due to many opportunities to learn the rigging, knots, and go down the tower, it was a very valuable school. I did well on the tower and lost no points during the grading period. You had to execute three rappels and do the correct procedure on each. If you forgot the correct procedure, you were out of luck and the points deducted.

The road march began early in the morning while it was still pitch black. You couldn't see the road to find your footing. My game plan was to run the first four miles, most of which was down hill, and then push as hard as possible to the turn around point at six miles. From that point I planned to run the next two miles down hill and push the last four to the finish.

The road march started and my plan worked well for the first three miles. I passed the majority of the marchers and felt strong. The road leveled out for the next two miles and then went one mile up hill to the turn around. At the five mile mark, the morning light was starting to peek through. I guess-timated I was in about tenth place.

During my push up the hill at a trot, I passed another half dozen marchers and finally made it to the turn around. I wasted no time and ran the one mile back down to mile seven. Now I was feeling some pain. There was a three-hundred meter steep grade to the flat stretch that hurt badly. Two marchers near me disappeared ahead of me. Once I got to the flat stretch, I ran for a half mile until I saw them again. When they walked … I ran.

When they ran ... I ran. I finished the road march number four out of the class and was pleased with my effort.

I graduated as the Distinguished Honor Graduate—number one in the class.

*   *   *

Chapter 9
Last Known Alive

Joint Field Activity 03-1C (first mission of the year 2003 in Cambodia) was to be my last mission to Southeast Asia. After I returned to Hawaii from Cambodia, I assumed my mission was complete. I then met with Lieutenant Colonel George, head of the JTF-FA Operations Directorate, who asked me to take the team again on 03-3L. I would lead a large team to investigate the loss of personnel from Lima Site 85 in Houaphan Province, Laos. This was the single biggest ground loss of Air Force personnel during the Vietnam War.

The investigation of Lima Site 85 had been on the docket since 00-3L. Continued delays by the Lao government had denied access to the area for three years. It was a very politically sensitive case and presented many physical challenges due to the site being located 5,100 feet atop a steep mountain named Phou (Lao word for mountain) Pha Ti. Many agencies and families would be watching this case develop. Lieutenant Colonel George told me JTF-FA had to send the "A" team to ensure it was a success.

Dr. Timothy Castle expertly laid out the events of Lima Site 85 in his book, *One Day Too Long*. It details the incredibly inept decision making of political and military leaders intent on keeping Lima Site 85 both operating and a secret. This attempt to retain the capabilities of Lima Site 85 would come at the expense of those men responsible for its operation. *One Day Too Long* is a compelling read and it details the history of the case to a point prior to my investigation.

03-3L would include a smaller docket of cases to ensure we had plenty of time for Lima Site 85. In preparation for these investigations, our team of analysts did extensive research and poured over vintage photos and survivor accounts. I personally focused on Phou Pha Ti and worked with the Intelligence section to find any clue to help determine the fate of the missing Lima Site 85 crew.

I spent exhaustive hours quizzing our intelligence analysts and becoming absolutely familiar with the facts. I also viewed a previous VCR tape of an investigation team searching the summit on rappel ropes. It was immediately apparent that the team did not go over the edge of the summit and limited their search due to the discovery of unexploded ordnance. The photos and video of the site depicted a very long vertical cliff face. It would take iron nerves to operate at that altitude and then go over the edge not knowing what would happen next. I knew exactly what operations at that altitude would look like. I had stepped off a similar ledge from an airplane over two hundred times and up to 25,000 feet. If you were not used to a birds-eye view, chances are you would not readily hang from a rope on the face of that mountain.

One report from a previous investigation team claimed they searched the first tree line below the cliff face by approaching from the bottom. Bill Gadoury was on that mission but on the top of the mountain. I asked him about it and he said the Assistant Team Leader had attempted to reach the bottom of the cliff but only had a period of hours to do it. Bill also said that during their climb they could not determine if they were in the correct area. This was the brightest part of our preparations so far. It was apparent that previous teams had not made it to the bottom of the cliff. Those teams were always pressed for time and it would take a team willing to go to the "edge" to bring back the evidence the families had been waiting for. This assumed there would be any evidence waiting to be found at the bottom of the upper cliff face.

Our preparations were complete and we were augmented with additional team members to a total size of seventeen personnel. This included three mountaineers from the U.S. Army Mountaineering School in Fort Wainright, Alaska, a Vietnamese Linguist, two debriefers, an Anthropologist, and recovery experts from the Central Identification Laboratory - Hawaii.

As usual, we assembled on deployment day at Hickam Air Force Base. After a round of goodbyes, it was time to load the airplane. As I headed to the departure gate Lieutenant Colonel George pulled me aside, looked me in the eye, and said, "This is the biggest case JTF-FA has ever done. No pressure!" I was amused by his sarcasm. Everything that the Lao Investigation Team had accomplished over the past three years came down to this investigation. This would be our defining moment during my tenure as Team Leader.

*   *   *

We arrived in Vientiane and had to conduct a series of interviews regarding Last Known Alive (LKA) cases. Then we would head north to Houphan Province. The Lao POW/MIA team provided a distinctly different level of cooperation between investigation of crash or burial sites and these LKA cases. The LKA cases were extremely emotional and involved known POWs that were held in Pathet Lao POW camps. There was much speculation as to why this lack of cooperation hung over the LKA cases. Our team had discussed this dynamic for endless hours, over three years of deployments, and we came up with a list of possibilities:

First, the current senior leadership in Laos was the very Pathet Lao soldiers who fought from the caves in Xam Nua. It was therefore highly likely they had direct knowledge of the fate of our POWs and did not want to be implicated in any negative effect from their recovery. Second, what if a POW was excavated that showed evidence of being executed? The Lao could be concerned of the potential for a public relations nightmare. Third, perhaps the Lao felt that if these emotional LKA cases were solved, the American public would lose interest in the issue and the international attention they received would end. Fourth, perhaps the Lao wanted to use the Trilateral method of involving Vietnamese witnesses to add plausible deniability to the fate of the servicemen. Fifth, the possibility that POWs, with valuable training and technical knowledge, had been taken to China and Russia. This was a very tangible and evidence-based theory. Sixth, there are still live POWs and/or MIAs in Laos today.

Often I have been asked to speculate on the possibility that American POW/MIAs were still alive in Laos. My opinion on the issue comes from my own experience and discussions with my team members. Environmentally, it is highly unlikely someone could survive without medical treatment to get them through bouts of the "funk." Dirty, musty, living conditions along with unsanitary food would surely sicken any prisoner at some point. Without medical attention, it is unlikely they would survive, and the medicines would have been reserved for the Pathet Lao and North Vietnamese soldiers. There could be anomalies to this speculation but they would definitely be the exception.

The more likely scenario would be a POW that had been held away from the Xam Nua area or taken away soon after capture. He would need to have some access to medical attention and be held in a remote area where he could maintain some quality of life. This is not a far-fetched idea. After the war, indoctrination camps were established where Lao citizens were held for many years and finally released to go home. Applying this similar scenario to POWs in a loose detention and survival could be possible. The last possibility was a prisoner had been held in loose detention and had now decided to remain in Laos. It was a plausible scenario supposing the POW had established a local family and lost touch with the reality of going home.

I have also been asked why the Lao would want to hold a live POW after all this time. Again, there is no answer that is not based on pure supposition. The potential political liability of a live POW being found would be immeasurable and therefore too dangerous. How could the lengthy detention or even presence of a POW/MIA in Laos, for over thirty years (minimum) be explained? The answer to that question would likely rest with the original issue. Not one American POW/MIA was *EVER* released from Laos. The reason could be political, cultural, a combination of both, or posturing for international recognition. It remains in the Lao best interest to ensure the stability and longevity of the POW/MIA "cash cow."

The bottom-line from a family's standpoint—show me the evidence! Until there is physical proof to include DNA testing there is still hope. To this day, families are still waiting, hoping, and depending upon the Defense POW/MIA Office, Joint POW/MIA Accounting Command, Stony Beach, and Central Identification Laboratory Hawaii, to bring their servicemen home. My team went to every extreme to produce result for the families. Nothing was to hard, too far, too high, or too dangerous. When safety was an issue, we just pushed harder. Our mandate came from the families and Ranger creed: "Never leave a fallen comrade."

*   *   *

O ur Last Known Alive (LKA) interviews in Vientiane started out with the same lukewarm response we had come to expect. We interviewed four cursory witnesses from a list of twenty that had been requested. Due to the poor cooperation being displayed by the Lao officials, the Detachment 3 Commander asked that I brief the American Ambassador to Laos on the Lima Site 85 investigation plan. I met with the Ambassador, briefed him on the plan and answered a few questions as to what we might encounter on the mountain. I also briefed him on the poor showing of Lao witnesses in Vientiane. He was very interested in this development. Apparently, there was a political tug of war underway with the Lao government and we had become involved.

After a four-day rain delay, we departed Vientiane for Xam Nua. When we arrived, we conducted coordination with Provincial and District officials, in Viengxai District, Laos. We would begin our stay in Xam Nua with the investigation of two

F-105 pilots shot down in 1967. The pilots were held in caves near Xam Nua by Pathet Lao forces.

During the three years from 00-4L to 03-3L, the Lao dragged their feet on these cases. They openly hampered the investigation of these cases to the point of being ridiculous. They denied the existence of caves in the area, even though they were clearly visible from the air. Then, in 2002, the IE was allowed to visit a very limited number of caves. This was not a significant concession since tourists could visit any number of caves they desired. Still the IE was allowed access to only a handful. While inspecting a few known caves, the IE ranged out and discovered a few more by cutting into the jungle to reach the base of the karsts. This surprised even the Lao officials who had no idea the caves were there.

A significant clue to the burial of at least one American was a caves' proximity to the location of the Non Kop marsh. There were reports of a nearby Non Kop Military graveyard. For two years, no one admitted knowing where it was located. Then on 00-4L, a local village chief led the team to the area located directly in front of the "Governor's" Cave. Directly in front of the cave, about 100 meters, was the military graveyard. The next logical step was to locate who cared for the graveyard to see if records existed of who was buried. Perhaps the caretakers had seen some evidence or had local knowledge that would be useful. For two years local officials claimed no one cared for the graveyard.

All these issues came to a head on 12 March 2003. The IE traveled with a retired Lao officer to Viengxai for one last attempt to locate the grave site. The team landed the Squirrel and MI-17 Helicopter in a rice paddy located between the village of Ban Bac and the "Friendship" cave. The entire area was quite small with around 400 meters between any one point in question.

Sammy and Jack during an interview.

The witness identified the cave as the one he had held the American in during the war. He then proceeded across the rice paddies to orient himself. The small knolls north and west of Ban Bac was identified as the area in which he claimed to have buried the American. The witness milled around for hours. Finally, he could not pinpoint a grave site. He did identify a one-hundred meter square area north of Ban Bac. It became apparent he was either disoriented, too old, or only had second hand knowledge of the incident. He may have attempted to deceive American teams for years.

This was my last trip and I had grown extremely frustrated with this orchestrated delay. It seems the Lao officials had toyed with my IE for the past three years. The idea that an American had to "investigate" to locate the burial site of these two lost Americans was ridiculous. This was a closed and controlled society and these Americans were known to be alive and in Pathet Lao custody. We had physical proof via vintage photographs. We also had transcripts of propaganda radio reports these prisoners were forced to make on Lao radio. The Pathet Lao definitely had these American prisoners and I wanted the officials to tell us where to find them. It was a frustrating situation.

We were not going to have a breakthrough in the investigation on this day. We loaded the Squirrel and MI-17 and began the flight back to Xam Nua. I was in the Squirrel and we would take the district officials back to Viengxai. As we flew over the Non Kop area, I looked down and saw a military detail clearing weeds and grass from the Non Kop graveyard. I pointed it out to the national official and requested to land. I wanted to see what military unit they were from for future investigations. The official refused. He tried to tell me it wasn't a graveyard. I animatedly told him I knew it was the Non Kop graveyard. He again refused and said he would inquire through provincial channels. This just compounded my frustration as I told him we had tried that for past two years. He still refused and looked away and out the window on the opposite side of the Squirrel. It would be a tenuous relationship during this series of investigations.

*   *   *

Chapter 10
The Sacred Mountain

Phou Pha Thi / The Sacred Mountain

Lima Site 85 has been one of the most controversial cases to consume the POW/MIA community. It involved the March 10, 1968 attack of Vietnamese Commandos against a radar site on a high mountain top karst named Phou Pha Ti, in Houaphan Province, Laos. This beacon and radar site was manned by nineteen Air Force Technicians who had clandestinely left the military to be aligned under a CIA cover company. Their operation provided an all-weather bombing capability which allowed American air power to bomb Hanoi even during the monsoon season.

Phou Pha Ti towering above Ban Louang village.

In response, the North Vietnamese Army began an offensive to remove Lima Site 85 from Phou Pha Ti. Hmong and Thai security forces under the direction of CIA advisors protected the approaches to the mountain. Early on the morning or 11 March 1968, twenty-five North Vietnamese Commandos climbed the cliffs of the western face and attacked and overran the site with grenade and machinegun fire. The next morning eight of the personnel were rescued by helicopter and the others have remained unaccounted. Later in the day, air strikes destroyed the radar equipment and survivor accounts led investigators to believe eight of the eleven remaining team members had been killed. What actually happened to these missing eleven became a huge mystery laced with conspiracy theories. Regardless, the families of the missing just wanted to know what had happened to their loved ones.

We flew to Ban Lauang village, a three-minute flight west of the top of Phou Pha Ti. There we cached fuel barrels that we would use to fill the Squirrel as needed. This allowed us to have less fuel on board and more weight allowance available to haul men and equipment. Also, it would allow the Squirrel to have more lift and maneuverability in the mountain winds.

Sheer limestone cliffs of Phou Pha Ti; Lima Site 85 center/top.

Our investigation plan we quite simple. We would search every nook and cranny of Phou Pha Ti near the old location of Lima Site 85. The Lao government had told JTF-FA that, in no uncertain terms, this would be our last chance to visit this mountain. Therefore, it was imperative we find the evidence if it was there to be found. To take advantage of every avenue, JTF-FA brought Vietnamese Trilateral witnesses who had participated in the assault on Lima Site 85. They would attempt to point out the locations where they had last seen American bodies. After the Trilateral portion of the investigation, my team had a free hand to search the mountain.

The top 1,000' of Phou Pha Ti in Houaphan Province, Laos.

On our first day on the mountain, we were permitted to begin our plans to search the summit area near the old Lima Site 85. Meanwhile, the Vietnamese veterans attempted to provide additional information as they oriented themselves to the area. We expected that after lunch they would be able to provide us some information on their knowledge of the final disposition of remains at the site.

Searching the backside of Lima Site 85.

Our Investigation Element occupied the morning by conducting a one-hundred meter line search to the northeast of the site and into a draw which some speculated could have remains. The search ended with negative results. The Doc and I also located and searched a tunnel that went into the mountaintop, dropped down to a second level, and then had a small body-sized opening in the mountain face. This was the second tunnel located. What made this tunnel interesting was that it had two levels and a living area in it. It was propped up by barrels and metal sheets from the old site and was a very secure location.

Vietnam veteran orients himself - members of DET 2 assist.

During the afternoon the witnesses provided various accounts of seeing American bodies at the site and helping to throw them over the cliff. Up to nine bodies were described with four possible locations from which they were deposited. The mountaineers then established safety lines in those locations from which to roll anatomically correct dummies over the side the next day.

The next day the team arrived on the site and immediately began preparations for the much anticipated drop of the dummies. Two video cameras were prepared and I explained the sites importance as it related to the case. One camera was located on the top of the mountain and the other camera was to be in the helicopter hovering off the face of the cliff. Site one was the Ops Van Boulders Ledge where up to seven Americans were thought to have fought, died and subsequently been rolled over the cliff. Site two was the Ops Van Ledge based on the description of a trilateral witness who said he rolled two bodies off at this site. The third site was the Tacan Ledge where two Americans were known to have died. One was blown over the ledge by a grenade and the other was last seen dead on the ledge.

With the dummies in place and safety ropes prepared to reach the edge we were prepared to go. I accompanied a Brown acting as the cameraman and Bob McElhinney piloted a Lao West Coast helicopter and hovered about three-hundred meters off the cliff face. I was connected by a hand held radio to MSG Collins who ran the show on the ridge. When all were ready, I told him to go ahead. He echoed "*Go Ahead*" in the radio and the first dummy rolled over the edge. I had a mental picture of what this event would look like but was totally surprised to see this dummy plummet unimpeded all the way to a ledge approximately seven-hundred feet below. I had totally expected it to at least bounce off a ledge or something on the way down but it just sailed to the bottom and impacted a ledge with a thud. You could just feel the thud as a puff of dust rose, and it continued to career down about another fifty meters until it came to rest on a lower ledge.

The second dummy consisted of a pair of heavy duty coveralls filled with sand and rice with all the seams sewed shut. All the dummies had blaze orange vests taped on to make them easy to watch and later locate. When this dummy rolled over the edge, he sailed about half way down that eight hundred foot face and then grazed a rock out cropping. The nick started to leak sand and it looked like it was trailing smoke. As it continued down it grazed more rocks and leaked more and more "smoke." Finally, the dummy disintegrated into a big poof of dust within fifty feet of the ledge. The last thing to be seen was the empty coveralls and orange vest floating into an adjacent treetop. Both of the first dummies landed within approximately thirty meters of each other.

Side view of Lima Site 85.

The third dummy was rolled off, fell about thirty feet and stopped. A mountaineer then rappelled down and rolled it off again. It went another fifty feet and stopped on another ledge. This told us what we needed to know. A body from this position likely would have come to rest on one of the many ledges on that side of the cliff face.

Marine SGT Traub searching the summit.

The team occupied the rest of the day by searching the summit down to the vertical face. It was accomplished by sending six team members laterally around the summit on safety lines of gradually longer length. I took the longest line of the day and got my first glimpse over the edge to see the many hidden ledges. There was every reason to believe that remains could be located on these ledges. I also got a good look at what could have been the Tacan Ledge—the ledge where five members fought and two died. This location could not be seen from the summit. Therefore, we took photographs of the ledge from the Squirrel. It was an exact fit of the site described by survivors from the incident.

Changing the plan with the mountaineers after a bad fall.

Two of the mountaineers attempted to reach what appeared to be a ledge, about three hundred feet below the south edge of the cliff face. The head mountaineer made it about 150 feet down when a large boulder came loose. The boulder and the mountaineer both began a tumble. The weight of the rock caused the rope to stretch as they plummeted. Once the climber separated from the falling rock he was snapped back upward. The resulting collision with the rock hurt the lead mountaineer's back. Both remaining mountaineers spent the rest of the day trying to get him over a reverse vertical edge. We were in danger of getting stuck on the mountain for the night because the rope the stranded mountaineer dangled upon had slipped into a crack in the rock. This prevented his being able to ascend over the edge. Finally, with another rope lowered to him, he was brought over the edge. That was our first day on Phou Pha Ti and we were already very lucky no one had been seriously injured.

Over the next week we continuously fought the low clouds to gain access to the mountain top. We would sit in the village and periodically fly the helicopter to the mountain to test the visibility. We used small windows when the clouds would clear from the summit to put three men at a time back on Lima Site 85.

SSG Raul Whitney, SSG Dylon Youngblood, and SSG Aaron Anderson - mountaineers suspending operations due clouds.

During this time, unknown to me, my wife had contacted Ann Holland. Ann's husband Melvin had been missing since the attack on Lima Site 85. My wife explained they had never met, but wanted to talk because I was on Phou Pha Ti. Ann was wary and somewhat skeptical after dealing with many false stories over the years. After she understood my wife's intent for calling, she asked her to tell me to look for Melvin's glasses. He always wore glasses.

It is times like this when you can believe in mystical elements or the intervention of a higher power or you can make your own luck. Either way, your burning desire to succeed overcomes all obstacles. I felt our team had lost its momentum due to injuries to two mountaineers, a failure to reach the first treeline and no evidence or remains being located during initial searches of the summit. Now weather restrictions threatened to seriously hamper any potential for success.

In a conversation with my wife, via satellite phone, I told her we were having difficulties on the mountain. I explained we were just getting started, and team members were getting hurt. After I ended our phone call, my wife called her mother in New Zealand to discuss this update.

In our next conversation, my wife told me her mother wanted me to talk to Phou Pha Ti. She instructed me to tell him, "Ruapehu from New Zealand says, Hello. Ruapehu also asks that you give up the men. Give them up so they can go home to their families." My wife went on to explain that Maori believe mountains are alive and can communicate with each other. I was skeptical, but my wife was adamant. "Promise me you will talk to Phou Pha Ti!" I promised I would and signed off for the night.

*   *   *

I looked toward the west and out across a huge expanse of jungle across the valley floor and across to the next range of mountains. This was rough and wild country and we were getting a panoramic view. I glanced to my right and watched as the mountaineers prepared the rope to go over the edge. They were inspecting the entire length to ensure there were no cuts or flaws and then coiling it in a big loop on the edge of the shelf.

600' upper vertical face of Phou Pha Ti

Yan walked up and surveyed the view. He said, "You think we should go for it?"

"Got no choice; we have to get down there somehow."

He suggested, "We could try from the bottom."

"They tried that in '96 and never made it." I replied.

"How are you gonna get off the ledge?"

"We'll figure that out when we get down there."

Yan let out a deep sigh and blew out a little air as he considered the situation. "Hmm, who's gonna go?"

I thought out loud, "I figured me, a mountaineer, and EOD."

Yan asked expectantly, "Want me to go?"

"No, you have to get us off the ledge."

We both dropped down to the upper ledge and I walked up to the edge and watched as the mountaineers talked about our options to get down the rock face.

I asked, "It's two-hundred meters down to the shortest part of the first ledge. How long is the rope?"

"Two-hundred meters," answered SSG Anderson with a smile on his face.

I asked, "Any chance of using two ropes for the safety of it?"

The head mountaineer, SSG Whitney chimed in, "No dice. The other two-hundred meter rope was damaged when the boulder fell on the chief mountaineer—when he tried to get on the ledge." Yan and I both let out a snort as we considered the options.

I suggested, "Well, let's throw the rope and see if it gets down to the ledge."

The mountaineer replied, "It'll need a weight to keep the wind from blowing it back into the face of the mountain."

I offered, "Here, use my rucksack."

In a matter of fact manner, SSG Youngblood said, "You know we're making a bit of history here."

Yan replied, "How's that?"

SSG Youngblood continued, "This will be a six hundred foot free rappel on one rope. We think that's the longest free rappel in Mountain Warfare School history."

Two more snorts from Yan and me.

It was time to get this task completed. I held my Motorola radio to my mount and said, *"Brown, this is the Major. Have the helicopter get into position."* We had a planned for the Squirrel to hover off the face of the mountain and watch the rope go down and ensure it would reach the next ledge.

I watched Bob steer the Squirrel to a hover off the face of the mountain. Brown radioed back, *"The helo is in position; give it a go."*

The SSG Anderson swung my rucksack back and forth to gain momentum and then gave it a heave out away from the face of the mountain. As it began its downward plunge, loop after loop of rope fed out of the big coil. It made a whirring sound that gained in pitch as the speed of the rope increased. In an instant the last loop was gone, the sound stopped, and the rope was taught. We all stood there wondering in our own minds if it had made it to the next ledge. A few seconds later, the answer came from my radio, "It is touching the next ledge; it is on the next ledge."

We identified three climbers who would make the rappel. They were a SSG Traub our Marine EOD expert from Okinawa, SSG Anderson the remaining healthy mountaineer, and myself.

The mountaineer went first and then it was my turn. I got hooked up and backed toward the edge. I quickly found that two-hundred meters of rope was pretty damned heavy to pull up with one arm to get the slack to rappel. The system we were using caused us to have to pull the rope up and force it through a ring in the middle of our abdomen. I didn't think about it ahead of time but multiple repetition of pulling up two-hundred meters of rope with one arm could be a challenge. The good news was you descended at your own pace and the system would prevent a catastrophic free fall to the bottom. The bad news was the pace was slow and with only one rope I was not confident of my life dangling on that single string. My concerns were compounded about one-fourth of the way down. The rope was rubbing on a weather sharpened ledge of rock.

There was nothing to be done at that point and I pulled up rope with vigor to get down as fast as possible.

Team Leader during rapell.

Once I got down to the ledge, I let the SSG Anderson belay SSG Traub. I was anxious to get a look at the ledge. Two things were immediately apparent—the entire ledge was rife with unexploded ordnance and rocks were coming off the top of the mountain like missiles. You could hear the faint whir of a rock cutting the air and building speed as it came down. It would ricochet off another rock near the bottom, go lateral to the ground, and smack into the trees or continue down the mountain. If one of those falling missiles hit one of the team members, it would seriously injure or kill him.

Unexploded Chinese Mortar Round

I moved along the rock wall to get out from under the rocks kicked loose by the next rappeller. I then stopped and extended a hand against the solid rock cliff face. I stared hard at the rock wall in front of me and said out loud, as if talking to a person and saying prayer at the same time, "Phou Pha Ti! Phou Ruapehu from New Zealand says hello. Ruapehu also told me to tell you to give up the men we are looking for—give them up so they can go home to their families." This was a moment where you felt the power and passion of your prayer. I felt a warm tingling as the hair rose on the back of my neck.

I then moved to find where the dummy had come to rest. As I tiptoed through the unexploded ordnance I noticed dark green cloth and pieces of trash and unidentifiable debris from the top of the hill. I dropped down the slope of the ledge about twenty meters. There I came upon the dummy laying in the area of

233

more pieces of cloth. Down another thirty meters I noticed the sole of a boot. Then what I had been praying for—a large sun bleached bone amongst fist- sized rocks. I let out a whoop that echoed down the mountain. I knew at a glance that the bone was likely a human leg bone. I had hunted and butchered wild and domestic animals and this was not from an animal. The worse case would be if it were from a Vietnamese or Lao soldier or another local villager. The bone was located in the vicinity of the boot and cloth and therefore I was both hopeful and optimistic

Clothing under the foliage.

By this time, all three climbers were on the ground and with just a cursory search we found survival vests, clothing and military sleeping bag pieces. All of this evidence was consistent with survivor accounts of the last night of the men on top of the mountain. They had started to receive artillery fire and climbed down the face of the mountain to sleep that night. They wore survival vests and had taken sleeping bags to stay warm. This was very significant. Everything pointed to the fact we had found at least part of the group we were looking for.

During this time, Bob was giving us hell over the radio about finding a place he could get us off the mountain. He piloted off the face of the mountain and kept an eye on our location. We continued along the face climbing very difficult ledges. Finally, we reached a rock outcropping which extended about fifteen feet from the face of the cliff. I guess-timated we could cut down a small tree in the way, clear some thorn bushes, and try to bring in the chopper.

During the cutting of the six inch diameter tree, the true precariousness of our situation became apparent. One slip and fall from this rock and you would likely fall another two-hundred feet to your death. Just hanging on to the rock to clear small bushes and trees was difficult. To step off the edge of that rock onto the skid would be risky. The hovering helicopter would bounce in the wake of his rotor wash and gusting mountain winds. This would be challenging even with a well-rehearsed and trained team.

Bob brought the Squirrel in toward the rock face and hovered about thirty meters out. He was bouncing up and down due to the turbulence of the rotor wash off the vertical face. We sat low and waited to see if this plan was going to work. After he got a feel for the winds, he slowly inched forward. I looked upwards and gave hand signals to let him know he had some distance between the front of the rotors and the rock face. He stopped with no more than two feet of clearance between the rotors and the sheer rock wall. Bob focused on keeping the Squirrel stable.

Trying to get off the ledge; me throwing a bag into the Squirrel.

One by one we gingerly stepped off the rock and onto the skid. That skid was two feet to the front of the rock and another two feet up. This step was complicated because you had to gradually apply your body weight while also slowly transferring from the safety of the rock to the skid. This gradual transfer of weight would leave you in a vulnerable position as you balanced between two points of safety. This gradual application of body weight was critical to allow Bob to compensate with the aircraft controls. There was no room for error with the front rotors literally inches from the rock face. A jump to the skid would cause the aircraft to buffet and likely crash down the mountainside. We successfully got all three of us onto the skid and the Squirrel slowly backed away from the mountain.

The day had been both dangerous and successful. We had reached a remote ledge with great potential that had never been visited before. We had also identified extreme risks to the team if we were to work on that ledge. Falling rocks, unexploded ordnance, treacherous terrain and no suitable landing/pickup zone—this was a very dangerous investigation indeed!

That night we ate dinner with Bob and discussed our plans for the next day. Before I could ask the possibility of being inserted back onto the ledge, Bob suggested that he could do it. He explained it was very tricky with the winds, rotor wash, and debris bouncing off the cliff face. Bob could account for these factors. His worry was the possibility of a sizeable rock falling from higher up the sheer cliff and directly into his rotors. That would be catastrophic.

After dinner, I sat with the anthropologist as he studied the large bone we found. He "supposed" it could be a monkey or goat or something. I think he might have been chiding or baiting me. This was serious business to me and I told him he had lost his mind. That was a human leg bone and that was all there was to it. He broke out his textbook and measured the width of the bone with a caliper. Then he looked back in the book and did it all over again. Finally I said, "C'mon Doc, say it ... you know it is ... say it."

Finally, he set the bone on the table and paused dramatically. He said the size and shape of the bone, compared to statistics and drawings in the reference text, was consistent with a mature non-Asian human. It was an upper thighbone and did not have an anomaly found in Southeast Asians. This anomaly was caused from a lifetime of squatting instead of sitting in a chair. That was a very big moment—both sad and gratifying at the same time. If the DNA testing confirmed our preliminary estimate it was likely we had found one of our missing comrades. The impact of a positive identification would bring both bad news and perhaps closure to one family. It would definitely provide the physical evidence to keep this investigation of Lima Site 85 open and active. Failure on this JFA could allow the case to be closed for lack of leads to pursue. We had what we had come for, but we also did not know which of the missing Lima Site 85 crew we had found.

Marine SGT Traub (EOD)(in blue cap) looking for UXO.

The next day we stopped at Ban Lauang to prepare for our lifts to the mountain. Each team member received a brief on the precariousness of the landing zone rock and practiced getting out on the skid as the Squirrel sat on the ground. We flew to the rock three at a time. I stepped out first and ensured each team member had a safety line tied around his waist. I locked into a tie-off point attached to a root and firmly grasped each safety line before each member stepped off the skid. We now had a well rehearsed drill to get in and out.

Master Sergeant Yan Collins leading the search of the ledge.

We took six team members, including one mountaineer, on the ledge and put the remainder on top to continue the search of the top and upper ledges. Our mountaineer on the lower ledge strung a lateral rope around the face of the mountain to have a tie-off and hand line.

This became necessary when I heard a scream, "I'm falling!" I turned around to see Sammy sitting on a semi-flat area slowly sliding downhill due to the loose round rocks. As I looked with a raised eyebrow, I could see Sammy was tied to a bush so there was no way he could possibly fall any farther. From that day on, we sent Sammy to the top of the mountain where it was safer.

Finding physical evidence of those that may have died on the mountain was only one facet of this investigation. We were also looking for any clue that a live POW/MIA could have been taken from the mountain. While most of the team was searching the ledge on Phou Pha Ti, our Stony Beach debriefers were staying on the top of the mountain or attempting to get to the nearby villages to interview anyone with knowledge of Lima Site 85. The Lao were not cooperative in allowing access to area villages but under daily pressure finally allowed an interview in two villages near the mountain. This again was halfhearted access to the witnesses and villages we needed to find to bring resolution to the investigation.

During this time Jack Johnson led a small team down the mountain to find a route to an LZ at the base. This could be used in an emergency or perhaps by a future excavation team. The team forged through vine-tangled thickets and rock drop-offs but identified a route. For two hours we pushed downhill. It would take at least three hours to trek upward along the same route. That would make it impractical for a future excavation team to utilize.

Each time I arrived on the mountain, I would wait until no one was watching and then talk to Pha Ti again. I was certain these little prayers were working because I had been very lucky in my searches. I found three Sears work boots and all five survival vests. Two of the boots were found far down on the second ledge. One day, Yan Collins saw me talking to the mountain and asked what I was doing? I explained to him what I had been instructed to do and how the Maori believed mountains could communicate. A few minutes later I looked over and Yan was talking to the mountain too.

The view upward from the ledge

Yan was a godsend, and I would have trusted him with my life at any point, and I did. We spent time on that ledge searching places we did not want any of the men to have to go. We picked our way together through areas covered with unexploded mortar rounds and cluster munitions. We trusted each other and we were both confident, strong, and had the stamina to push hard under the relentless sun and heat on the face of that mountain.

The mountaineers could not reach some ledges about one-hundred feet up from the upper ledge, so Yan and I free climbed up to the ledge to ensure we didn't leave someone behind up there. It was tricky as grass had grown on these ledges and it was difficult as times to get a handhold. I had found a good-sized ledge slightly farther up, so I searched it and then climbed back down.

Unexploded rocket hiding under the leaves.

We thought it was hard going up. It was even more difficult climbing down. The hand and footholds were hard to identify and the slippery vegetation made it very precarious. It was dangerous but manageable until Yan lost his grip, slid and during the fall managed to get to a small ledge where he hurt his back. We picked our way down together and made it back to the upper ledge.

BLU-26 cluster mines nestled in the foliage.

As we sat with the team on the upper ledge, a mountaineer was coiling some rope for a hand line. I glanced over and saw him standing on a BLU-26 cluster munitions and commanded him, "DON"T MOVE!" Next I said, "EOD." The Marine Sergeant walked over, picked it up carefully and took it over to an area between the rocks where we had started to consolidate the unexploded munitions. Right then I decided we had pushed our luck to the point that it was only a matter of time until someone was hurt. We had done our best here and it was time to get off the mountain and present the evidence to Joint Task Force Full Accounting to let them decide the feasibility of bringing an excavation team to the mountain.

The team searched the entire area of Phou Pha Ti Lima Site 85 over a sixteen-day period between 14 and 29 March 2003. The search included all areas of the summit, cliff face, and ledges of Lima Site 85 and any other areas we felt had the possibility of being pertinent to the investigation.

Each night I religiously made an entry in my personal log of the days events. It was a habit I had gotten into during this tour of duty. All our searching resulted in a variety of evidence from the different areas we searched.

Survival Vest found on the ledge.

On the summit that had once been the site of the vans, generators, and TACAN beacon, we collected many pieces of bone (osseous material) but our anthropologist inspected them closely and determined they were not human. We found caves in the Northeastern draw. Doc and I inspected a large two-level cave that came to an opening overlooking the valley. This was definitely not the one discovered on 98-5L. The entry had recently been uncovered as the grass was still matted and there was dirt on the rocks. It looked as though someone had just discovered it from a cliff side entry and unearthed it. The length of the tunnel was about fifteen meters and had barrels and steel grating reinforcing it. A tight squeeze between some grating and you entered a second room at a lower level. At the end of that room was a one-meter wide hole looking out onto the cliff face. There was no evidence of remains in the cave. During the search of the summit, the team found a U.S. canteen and some cloth.

Remnants of a Sears boot found on the ledge.

The search of the upper ledge produced considerable evidence including possible remains, clothing fragments, boot soles, five survival vests, a canteen, a CAR-15 magazine, and a sleeping bag zipper. What was interesting about these survival vests was that some of them had actually grown up into the trees about ten feet from the ground. Over the years the upward motion of the tree just raised the vest with it.

On the lower ledge we found more evidence that included four SEARS work boots in three different sizes.

Lower LZ where Bob hated to go. The debris would travel up a vertical wall to the front and back down into the rotors.

On 27 March I rappelled into the northwestern watershed with Brown and Carbonell and searched the area with no results. It was a very rough boulder field and any evidence could easily have been underneath the rocks. We free climbed out and made our way to the lower LZ. This was all very grueling and took a lot out of us to make our way from one watershed to the next.

MSgt Giovani Carbonell searching the northwestern draw.

On our last days, the team searched a draw on the northwestern side of the cliff face and discovered a small cave about thirty meters from the top where there were the remnants of a survival knife. There was no way to tell if this was significant because the Vietnamese and Lao had been here for over thirty-five years. We had done our job and now it was time to go home!

The top of Phou Pha Thi was searched thoroughly on this mission for remains and life support items with no luck. Numerous UXOs were located on the top; most of the munitions did not contain fuses. The ones that were live were marked with a red flag. The life support items and possible remains for this mission were found off the west side of the cliff. This area also contains numerous fully functional UXOs with many still containing safety pins. The UXO discovered included: 2.75" and 3.5" White Phosphorous rockets with warhead, 60mm High Explosive (HE) mortar rounds, Chi Com Stick Grenade, 3.5" WP, 81mm HE/Illumination rounds, BLU-26 anti-personnel mines, Rocket Propelled Grenade (RPG) warheads, 82mm mortar rounds, 57mm HE rounds, Claymore mine (pieces only), 4.2" HE/Illumination, and MK-82 (500lb bombs) with time/fuse.

For a Recovery Element to work in the area UXOs were just one threat to consider. Working below a two-hundred meter cliff on a steep angle with washouts flowing into forty-foot cliffs just enhanced the UXO dangers. Rock slides and falling rocks were caused by the workers simply moving around. This drastically increased the chances of detonating one of the many UXOs. The shifting rocks for personnel traversing the ledges resulted in UXOs surfacing from a semi-buried position. If a Recovery Element in this area is approved, the team should be carefully chosen. Even then the risks may outweigh the results. The costs and the risks along with the constant weather delays and extremely dangerous access to this site would hamper any chance of running a safe and effective full-blown recovery.

*   *   *

Messages Home

22 MAR 03 2000 Hrs:

We had a good day on Phou Pha Ti today and I think Pha Ti helped me again. I talked to him today and I asked him to tell me where to look. We searched for a few hours and found nothing and then I figured since I had time I would go find the radio I dropped four days ago. I had decided not to get it then because it had fallen too far down and it would be dangerous. For some reason today I just decided to go. It sounds like bullshit but I climbed 40 meters down to my radio and when I saw it, it was laying right next to a survival vest (within one foot). There is absolutely no doubt in my mind that Pha Ti is helping me. I have found all four vests now and how else could you explain it.

That means we have located evidence that at least four guys were in that drainage and perhaps more. The best thing is when Pha Ti guided me to that last vest it was on the last possible ledge before another 500' vertical drop. I think he wants me to look on the next ledge down. I can "feel" there is something there. He is definitely giving me guidance ... I believe it and I think that opens the door to his help.

23 MAR 03 2040 Hrs:

We had another good day today since we found the boots. It is sad in one way but good in the fact that we have some proof that might help these guys get home. It is too bad for the families that they didn't send this team over here years ago because we are defying the different risks involved by doing the job methodically and professionally. I wish they had sent me 10 years ago when the evidence would have been more fresh and the wives and survivors still alive to see the end of the puzzle.

26 MAR 1950 Hrs:

Whoa, what a day. We got shit loads of work done and I really got drained from walking and walking and climbing and whew!!! The only real success came today from the mountaineers who found a boot sole on a ledge below the Tacan Ledge. I am not all that excited though because the tread pattern is different from others we have found. The good news is we have another clue as to a place we need to re-search. MSG Collins found two large caves on a ledge, which he will inspect tomorrow. I still think something else good is going to happen. We just need to figure out how to get down to two remote areas and onto some ledges the mountaineers are having trouble with. I hope we can find some more clues on this one.

Last Message Home:

Right now it is 0300 for you on a Saturday morning and I need to get some sleep because I am drained from today. We had high drama trying to get off the ledge with rain coming in and almost no visibility. We made it and we were very lucky. We aren't going there again since we have pushed our luck too far. The other thing laying right next to the vest today was an unexploded mortar round. There is unexploded ordnance all over that site. Also, falling rocks, a dangerous LZ, huge drops, it is a dangerous place but we are done with it. Thank you Pha Ti!!!!!

* * *

Answers

Our search of Phou Pha Ti did not provide immediately conclusive evidence to the fate of the eleven missing servicemen on the mountain. Additional Recovery and Investigation operations would be required. A Recovery Element would be required to get on that upper ledge and search under the upper level of fist sized rocks for additional remains. Also, pending DNA testing on the large bone we recovered would determine the possible identity of at least one of the missing.

There were signs that other people had been to the ledge before us. There was one half inch thick small tree that had been cut with a machete. It was black from years in the elements and was sure evidence others had beat us there. It was likely local villagers or soldiers who had taken the time to find a route from the bottom. It could have been local villagers had reached that ledge scavenging larger pieces of remains for their potential monetary worth or use in primitive local medicinal concoctions. Regardless, the evidence would indicate someone would have taken all items of value from that ledge. Yet, we found five survival vests in good shape. Some of the boots were ripped open from the sole. None of the intact boots had any bones inside. The evidence suggested the area had been sterilized before our arrival. Only one sizeable bone had been found and this was likely an oversight of those who had sterilized the area.

The most positive fact for a future excavation was that no scavenging could effectively remove the small bones forming the hands and feet. They would still be there under the upper stratus of rock, foliage, and debris. A future excavation team will likely be able to find the evidence the families await.

The likely removal of remains from the mountain will confuse attempts to account for all the missing from Lima Site 85. One could speculate the removal of the remains was for the specific purpose to cloak evidence of survivors taken from the mountain.

Our investigation team was denied free access to the villagers of Ban Lauang. Those villagers were the most likely scavengers of Phou Pha Ti. Also, because of their close proximity they could hold critical clues to the fate of any live Americans after the Vietnamese raid on Lima Site 85.

A final dinner for a successful and safe investigation.

The investigation of this case needs to continue. It is likely that key Lao and Vietnamese officials hold the answer to what happened to the remainder of that team from Lima Site 85. I wish we could have provided finality based on physical proof for all of those families that have been waiting so very long for resolution. The quest would need to continue, but the Joint POW/MIA Accounting Command would have to spearhead the search.

* * *

After our return to Hawaii, my team gave a brief to Brigadier General Redmann with other key command members in attendance. During the brief, Gen Redmann asked me pointedly why I went down the rope on a two-hundred-meter rappel. I immediately looked around the room to see where that question would have been generated. I had the utmost respect from General Redmann and knew that question must have been planted in his ear. This would be his way of providing me the opportunity to address an unknown issue. It never ceased to amaze me that no matter how successful my team had been, there was always a subversive shadow of deceit nipping at us. That was the way personalities in this POW and MIA business jockeyed for stock and position.

I knew that I was a Certified Rappel Master, refreshed my training while graduating as the distinguished honor graduate of the Army Air Assault School, and was trained in mountain climbing techniques as an Army Ranger. Someone was likely enjoying this moment and I did not want to enhance their sense of glee. Therefore, I opted to provide the shortest explanation. I only responded by saying that I was an Army Ranger and I knew what I was doing.

Chapter 11
Day of Reckoning

In June 2003, before my departure from JTF-FA, I was asked to brief the American League of Families in Washington D.C. on the investigation of Lima Site 85. Each year the U.S. Government flew the family members of the missing to a conference. There they would be provided updates on their individual cases and a briefing of progress within the entire POW/MIA arena. I traveled there with a small team from JTF-FA which included BG Redmann.

We arrived at the hotel and set up a display table opposite the conference room. This was a prime location as all family members could stop at our table and ask questions. As the conference progressed, the family members passed by but seemed to shy away from my table. I decided to break the ice by asking each passerby why they were at the conference.

That is how I met Trish Burnett. She was walking down the hallway while glancing at the tables but did not appear to know exactly what she was looking for. When she neared our table, I asked if she was there for the conference. Trish confirmed she was. I then asked what country her loss dealt with. She explained her father had been lost in Laos. I had worked all investigations in Laos for three years and was surprised when her case number was not on the top of my head. I knew by the number sequence that it was likely a helicopter and in Savannakhet province. I looked at the case background in my computer data base and realized that her father had crashed on a small hilltop. I had driven by and flown that site many times during other investigations. I had actually referenced that site while researching other cases.

There were many helicopters that had crashed in Laos along Highway 9 during the Lam Son Offensive in 1971. The raid involved American aircraft and pilots ferrying South Vietnamese infantry out of Vietnam and about twenty-five miles into Laos. The objective was to seize Ban Xepon. Xepon was a small village at the crossroads of supply routes used by the North Vietnamese.

Xepon Church – Lao monument to the defeat of the Lam Son offensive – two miles west of Xepon.

The North Vietnamese fought back hard and stalled the offensive. South Vietnamese units then attempted to retrograde back to the border. Individual units were stranded and U.S. aircrews and helicopters flew hundreds of harrowing missions in an attempt to extract South Vietnamese troops. Many of these stranded units were located on plateaus and firebases in the valley. Much of my team's time over the prior three years was spent trying to locate the crash sites and find evidence of the crews of some of the 168 helicopters lost during this effort. This was the same offensive which generated the case Earl Swift had pursued in his book. Colonel Sheldon Burnett was a member of one of those crews. I quickly reviewed the circumstances of loss while Trish waited.

Circumstances of loss: (Courtesy P.O.W. Network):

Randy Ard had been in Vietnam only a few weeks when an emergency call came in for him to fly the squadron commander to a platoon command post to work his way down to his Third Platoon, which was in ambush in the northwest segment of South Vietnam.

He flew his Kiowa Scout chopper from the 5th Mech and picked up a passenger, LtCol. Sheldon Burnett, the squadron commander; Capt. Phil Bodenhorn, Alpha Company commander; and SP4 Mike Castro, Third Platoon RTO. Ard mistakenly flew past the command post and west into Laos. Seeing yellow marking smoke, he took the chopper down lower. It was too late to pull up when they heard the sound of an RPD machine gun and AK-47's. They had been tricked into a North Vietnamese ambush. The helicopter went down fast, and smashed into the brush, coming down on its side (or upside down, depending on the version of the account).

Ard and Burnett were trapped in the wreckage, but alive. Ard got on the radio and began mayday calls. Bodenhorn and Castillo, who had been in the rear seat, got out of the aircraft. Bodenhorn managed to free Art, but he had two broken legs and possibly a broken hip. Burnett was completely pinned within the wreckage and injured, but alive. Bodenhorn and Castillo positioned themselves on opposite sides of the aircraft for security and expended all the colored smoke grenades they had, marking their position for rescue

Bodenhorn and Castillo soon heard North Vietnamese approaching, and killed these Vietnamese. The two listened for nearly an hour as others advanced towards their position from two directions, and 155 artillery rounds impacted very near them. They couldn't understand why they were not being rescued, unless it was because the enemy was so close to them. A helicopter flew over, but took heavy fire and left. They decided to leave Ard and Burnett and escape themselves. They told Ard, who nodded wordlessly. Burnett was drifting in and out of consciousness. Both men were alive.

Bodenhorn and Castillo worked their way to 80 yards away when a UH1C came in on a single run, firing flechette rockets which seemed to explode right on the downed chopper. Later, they watched an F4 roll in for a one-bomb strike over the crash site. Ard and Burnett were surely dead. Bodenhorn and Castillo were rescued by ARVN troops an hour later. Ard and Burnett were classified Missing in Action.

Trish Burnett and I talked about the type of terrain in the crash area, the status of her father's case, and the investigations that had taken place by previous teams. She explained that she was four years old when her dad went off to war and he never came back. After her mother had passed away, she had taken a lead role for her family to keep looking for her dad.

I was irritated that I had not had the chance to investigate Colonel Burnett's case and took a specific interest. I read her files and used my experience in Laos to coach her to ask the right questions. I told her the right people to talk to and how to be a "squeaky wheel" to ensure her fathers' case was expeditiously investigated. I also talked with Bill Forsythe in the analysis section about the fact Colonel Burnett was last known to be alive. That meant this case should have been a first priority.

JTF-FA was giving her case equal attention, but it took time to get the right witnesses, be in the right place, and end an investigation successfully. To make it worse, Colonel Burnett's case involved Trilateral witnesses who were Vietnamese veterans. This required coordination between Laos, Vietnam and the U.S.—that effort was extensive and could experience many delays. Many families waited patiently—others were more aggressive. Sometimes even a nudge could help get a case added to a specific Joint Field Activity. This case was added to the next case load in Laos.

I stayed in touch with Trish and talked with my old Team Sergeant, Suriyan Collins, before and after the investigation. The investigation happened just after my departure from JTF-FA. Yan was very confident they had the right location of a burial site based on a key witness. Yan was correct and a successful excavation ensured COL Burnett finally returned home to his family. Colonel Sheldon Burnett is now buried in Arlington Cemetery.

Just prior to the ceremony at Arlington Cemetery Trish called me in Hawaii. The Burnett family was making the final preparations for the ceremony. I was happy for the family and glad to have helped in even a small way.

*   *   *

Imet multiple families who had lost their loved ones in Laos and Cambodia and were hungry for any information regarding their lost family members. It was eye-opening to see first-hand the void of information that had reached the families over the years. These people waited in an enduring state of trust and dependency on U.S. government efforts to locate information on their loved ones. Almost three decades had passed and the information still came at a slow trickle.

What became very apparent to me was the major cultural difference in the view of family members of servicemen from the military versus the political sides of the issue. In the Army the needs and security of the family is equally as important as that of the serviceman. Within the POW/MIA issue the serviceman was missing and the needs of the family shifted to a back seat.

A middle-aged man in a suit walked up to the table and said he was attending the conference because his wife had lost her brother in Laos. I asked him what case it was and he replied it was Case 1430. I was surprised because I knew this case very well since we had located and surveyed the crash site. I told him I had been there just months before and could tell him all about it. His jaw dropped and he walked away without saying a word. Moments later he returned and introduced his wife Sharon Blackman. She explained that her brother's name is LT Vincent Calvin Scott Jr. He was an Air Force pilot shot down in Laos. Each year they attended the conference in hopes of hearing any news on the progress in his case. They asked me to tell them anything I could because they had never talked to anyone who had been to the area where LT Scott was reportedly lost. As we talked I reference the background information on the case in my data base to refresh my memory. LT Scott was listed as:

Date of Loss: 22 April 1969.
Country of Loss: Laos.
Status (in 1973): Killed In Action/Body Not Recovered.
    Crash site; Killed; Xekong Province; Kong River; Missing;
    Aircraft downed.
Circumstances of loss:
    On 22 April 1969, the two-man crew of a F-4D were in the number one aircraft of two on a combat mission over Laos. The case aircraft rolled into attack a truck park and crashed during the bombing run. The wingman observed a large fireball on the ground - no beeper or voice contact was established. Search and Rescue was not initiated due to the terrain and heavy enemy activity in the area.
        (Courtesy POW/MIA Net)

This was a case that we discovered with our freelance style of investigation and I remembered it well. It was a big find for our team that did not come without an equally large challenge. I then described in detail the mountaintop crash site we had visited and the three days of searching through thick jungle and vertical cliff areas.

Our team flew to the record loss area of the case and conducted a reconnaissance flight of a sizeable mountain bordered on the north side by the Xekong River. On the east and south sides were two separate villages. As we hovered over the village to the south, I noticed it was not referenced on my military map. I talked into my boom mike and told Erik to land at the village below us. Erik was always eager for something new and began to circle down. The Lao National Official in the back seat of the Squirrel began to stop us. He then sat back and decided to let us proceed.

We landed just to the south of the village and along a small creek. Immediately, villagers emerged from the thick brush separating the village from the stream. They gathered around with great interest. They were more primitively dressed than many villagers we encountered. They wore headbands, sarongs, and the women were topless. Since we were always on the prowl for aluminum aircraft parts, we noticed numerous villagers were inhaling from bongs. Little kids and old adults alike had bongs made of bamboo and aluminum. Whatever they were smoking, it was surely addicting. None of the villagers could take the pipe away from their mouths and they had no interest in sharing.

We interviewed a group of village elders while squatting in a circle behind the MI-17. Two of the witnesses immediately confirmed they had a crash site on the mountain towering above their village. They confirmed the general date of the crash and said they watched the incident take place. One witness recounted seeing Vietnamese anti-aircraft guns firing at the airplane that exploded and crashed on the crest of the mountain. The villagers did not visit the site until after the war to search for wreckage. They found considerable aircraft wreckage spread across the mountain and down the north and south slopes. They also claimed to have seen uniform, boot, and bones. They claimed to have left the bones alone because of cultural taboos. Their beliefs in these taboos were very powerful and bad karma and ghost haunting were a pervasive fear. I asked if another team had ever been to their village. They said they had seen us fly over for years. Each time they would say, "There go the bone hunters." They were glad we finally stopped.

There were no landing zones on this mountain. Two plainly visible heavily scarred areas of jungle ran down the southern slope. The villagers claimed these were created by landslides which were later overgrown. Erik steered the Squirrel in close to the thickly vegetated scars. The rotor pushed the canopy downward and we could jump off the skid from about ten feet.

As usual, I was first off the skid and dropped to the ground. We lowered two saws immediately and I was followed by Adam Pierce. Another lift of team members came in and we made our way up the ridge. Adam then took a detail to cut an extraction LZ near the summit. There would be no way to get back into the helicopter off the slope we had entered on.

View toward Vietnam from the top of the ridgeline.

Right at the crest of the ridgeline and near the summit was a large and heavy piece of wreckage. Nearby was a small pile of assorted metal pieces. We continued on and began a search that easily located numerous pieces of aircraft wreckage. Serial numbers were extracted that correlated to an F-4 Phantom but not to a specific type of F-4.

Slowly we began to piece together a likely scenario for the

events of that fateful day. This narrow ridgeline overlooked a ford on the Xekong River far below. American aircraft were attacking the North Vietnamese convoys which were vulnerable while traveling on rough trails winding down treeless slopes immediately to the northwest. There were fighting positions dug along our ridgeline and a larger position right at the vicinity of the crash site. This would have been to house a crew-served heavy machinegun or anti-aircraft gun with an unobstructed view to engage incoming aircraft. We surmised that LT Scott in his F4D Phantom fighter jet had been attacking the ford and was engaged by the enemy positions on the ridgeline. The evidence suggested he had attempted to engage the enemy heavy weapons position which resulted in a fateful dual that both sides likely lost. There was no other explanation or reasonable probability that the F-4 would impact on this isolated and specific enemy position on the lip of a very narrow ridgeline.

I then decided it was time to search the near vertical face of the mountain as there was wreckage that had fallen down that very steep slope. SSG Josh Toone, our Explosive Ordnance Disposal (EOD) Technician, and I began to pick our way down the drop-off. As our EOD rep, SSG Toone was ecstatic after he came across an unexploded bomb and stopped to give it a worthy inspection. Just down from the summit I came across a red colored piece of wreckage with a serial number I had never seen before. It would turn out to be a piece of radar equipment found only on an F-4D.

During this same time, we located one of the aircraft engines four-hundred meters down the opposite slope. We connected the dots from this engine and suspected impact point and searched the area for the next three days. It was grueling but we hacked our way through the thick jungle to effectively search this area. In the end, we knew the type of aircraft, but had no physical proof the crew had died on that mountain.

We gathered as a team at the original pile of wreckage found at the crest. Our team conference concluded that we had done what we could with this site. During our discussion, MSGT Howie Mariteragi, our Life Support Technician, continued to inspect small pieces of metal from the pile. With each small piece he used a metal brush to scrub away corrosion. No sooner had the team decided we had completed our mission, than Howie announced, "Wait!" Proudly, he held up a two inch by 3/8-inch piece of metal and said the magic letters, "MBES." That meant Martin Baker Ejection System (MBES) and provided physical proof at least one member of the crew was in the aircraft at the time of impact.

The Blackman's hung on my every word and were utterly grateful for the information I had for them. I explained that we were *just lucky*. After we landed in the village not depicted on my map, the witnesses said, "Yeah, we know of a crash site. We have seen you fly over for years but no one ever stopped at our village." It was just a matter of stopping and asking.

I stayed in touch after the conference and made sure they received some photos of the area to have something tangible when they talked about LT Scott.

*   *   *

A young man with his son walked by and I asked a similar question. He explained his brother had crashed in Cambodia and he told me his case number. By chance, I had been there just three months before and again explained our investigation of the site and what we had found.

I vividly described the helicopter crash site, the tree it crashed into, the spread of the wreckage and the pieces of flight suit and other evidence we found there. We discussed the search and rescue attempt of a medic being lowered in on a sling and attempting to attend to the crew. He stayed until North Vietnamese soldiers approached when he fired his .45 caliber pistol before being hoisted out again. Everything we had seen was consistent with that account to include a .45 caliber spent shell casing I had recovered. Again, he was very grateful and they walked away.

On the second day of the conference, this same man and his son walked up to the table and showed me a vintage photo of a Vietnam era pilot standing next to his helicopter. He went on to explain that the photo was taken just before his brother left on his mission—he never came back.

That was a powerful moment for both of us, as we stood together with him holding a picture of his brother standing next to the aircraft. This was the man whose pieces of flight suit I had handled and aircraft wreckage we had inspected. I was the closest he had been to his brother since the day he went to war.

*   *   *

Investigations in Southeast Asia were generally non-emotional—except you knew you were looking for someone's family member and your brother-in-arms. At the front of every case folder was a photograph of the missing to remind you of who you searched for. You empathized with the service member you were looking for. In many instances you put yourself in his position, or the enemy's, to look for clues: *"Where would I go? What would I do? Where would I take him?"*

This conference brought it all home because you were face to face with the family member. The family member with the emotional attachment to the service member for whom you had searched. Also, the family member who hung all their hopes on the work you had conducted—they totally depended upon you to bring their loved ones home.

There were some tears shed as I talked with some family members. You could feel their frustration and desire to bring closure—good or bad, to their situations. Some families still hoped for missing service members to come home alive. Others resigned themselves to the likelihood their loved one was no longer alive — they just wanted them to be brought home for burial. Closure for each family is a private and individual thing.

On the second day of the conference, I had the privilege to conduct a presentation to the group on my team's efforts on Phou Pha Ti. I was proud of what we had accomplished. I emphasized that my team had gone to every effort, in every investigation, to run every lead to its end. We did the best job possible.

After the presentation, many family members expressed their gratitude for our efforts. I finally had the chance to sit down with Ann Holland and have a private conversation. I assured her that our team had done everything possible to bring her husband home. We had done our best, but we had not found the clues we needed. We had only provided a piece of the puzzle.

*   *   *

My tour at JTF-FA had been a rewarding and successful one. The Lao and Cambodian villagers called us "The Bone Hunters." We nicknamed ourselves "The Clean-up Crew." We had success where teams before us had failed. In all, we found or resurveyed twenty-six previously undiscovered crash sites in three years. We recommended twenty-three for excavation and this brought the number of missing crash sites to under thirty in Laos. Those twenty-three crash sites had over fifty associated fellow brothers-in-arms on board. Years of excavations and DNA testing will bring these heroes home.

Noteworthy discoveries of our team were: the last Jolly Green Giant (HH-34) helicopter and crew missing in Southeast Asia; the last National Guard pilot and his crew missing in southeast Asia; results at Phou Pha Ti after previous teams had failed; finding Governor Howard Dean's brother and his Australian travel buddy Niel Sharman; locating the pilot of an A-6 fighter located on a mountaintop 80 kilometers from where he had been thought to be lost; locating "Earth Quake McGoon", an Air America pilot missing since 1957 while attempting to resupply the French siege at Bien Dien Phu; solving the mystery after my erroneous basis for "Where They Lay,"; and most importantly helping bring a bit of bittersweet closure to as many families as we could during my tenure. I was privileged to have worked with a talented and dedicated team who had an enduring impact on this honorable mission to find our missing comrades.

My time in search of our POW/MIAs lost in SEA generated so very many stories. Should I tell the one about the Green Beret who was shot in the chest and buried? We came back and found his gravesite on a forested knoll. The trees were still scarred from the firefight that occurred that day. Maybe the one about the O-2 Spotter plane that we found along a river in Xekong Province that involved stories about how a cowboy boot wearing pilot was shot down. We found his crash site with evidence from an engine data plate on a remote ridgeline. Then there was the search in Thailand and Cambodia for an F-111 Bomber that took off from Thailand and disappeared. Or flying to Kotang Island off Cambodia to search for Marines lost in the Mayaguez Incident. There are just too many stories to tell.

*   *   *

Enduring Freedom

I departed Joint Task Force – Full Accounting and deployed with the 25th Infantry Division (Light) to Operation Enduring Freedom in Afghanistan. I had a final opportunity to make my contribution to the war on terrorism. This would be the last noteworthy event in my Army career that had begun with the notion of a four year tour in the Army Rangers. It ended twenty years and nine days later after an unexpected odyssey.

I made my contribution to secure America, just like millions of other Americans. Like my brothers-in-arms, I had sacrificed a major portion of my life: relationships, marriages, anniversaries, birthdays, special holidays, and all those simple things we take for granted. I can sleep well knowing our country remains secure and in the hands of another generation of fighting men.

Three months before I retired I received an email asking if I would be interested in returning to Afghanistan as a military contractor and advisor. I would be a strategic planner for Combined Forces Command – Afghanistan … again. I thought it over for a day and replied that I could not wait.

After all, I was feeling lucky … I had always been lucky … I had Thick Luck!

"BOUNA"

Epilogue

In February 2006, I sent an email message to Ann Holland just to say hello and let her know that my wife and I were thinking about her. I had not seen her since our short visit in Washington, D.C. at the POW/MIA Conference. To read the text left me in a small state of shock because time had distanced me from the families and issues of the search for our POWs and MIAs.

17 February 2006:
In case you haven't heard, the bone you found 3 years ago was finally I.D.'d in November. It was Pat Shannon. His wife died about 6 months before the I.D. was made. He has 3 adult kids in Oklahoma City. They are having the services on April 15. I am going to try and make it. It may be the only one they have for any of the guys left behind on the mountain. Someone at DPMO told one of the Shannon daughters they will go back to the hill one more time then they will have a group burial at Arlington, no matter what they find. They want to close the case. So Thank You, thank you, thank you for helping to bring Pat home to his family.

This message enforces the fact that the families of the missing are still waiting. They still depend on JTF-FA (now the Joint POW/MIA Accounting Command) to bring them home.

Glossary

Abbreviations/Acronyms

1SG	First Sergeant
A-10	Thunderbolt Tank Buster
ABN	Airborne
AC-130	Spectre Gunship
AH-6	Little Bird helicopter
AIT	Advanced Individual Training
ARS	Army Reception Station
ASVAB	Army Service Vocational Aptitude Battery
BABC	Ban Alang Base Camp
BDU	Basic Duty Uniform
BLU-43	Dragon Tooth anti-personnel mine
BMP	Tracked Russian armored personnel carrier
BRDM	Wheeled Russian armored personnel carrier
BT	Basic Training
C-130	Hercules transport plane
C-141	Star lifter transport plane
CH-47	Chinook helicopter (cargo/troops)
CH-53	Pavlo helicopter (cargo/troops)
CAR-15	Carbine Assault Rifle
COL	Colonel
COLT	Combat Observation Lasing Teams
CPH	Copper Head laser guided artillery round
CPT	Captain
CO	Commanding Officer
DAP	Direct Action Penetrater (MH-60 Helicopter)
DIA	Defense Intelligence Agency
DivArty	Division Artillery
DPMO	Defense POW/MIA Office

DZSO	Drop Zone Safety Officer
FIST	Fire Support Team
FO	Forward Observer
FRAGO	Fragmentation Order
FSB	Forward Staging Base
FSO	Fire Support Officer
FTX	Field Training Exercise
G/LVVD	Ground Vehicular Laser Locator Designator
GTMO	Guantanamo Bay, Cuba
HALO/	High Altitude Low Opening/High Altitude High
HAHO	Opening
HIND-D	Russian Attack Helicopter
ID	Infantry Division
IE	Investigative Element
ISB	Initial Staging Base
JMPI	Jumpmaster Parachute Inspection
JFA	Joint Field Activity
JOTC	Jungle Operations Training Center
JRTC	Joint Readiness Training Center
JSOC	Joint Special Operations Command
JTF-FA	Joint Task Force Full Accounting
KILO	Impact area on Fort Benning, GA
LAW	Light Anti-tank Weapon
LBE	Load Bearing Equipment
LCM	Mechanized Load Carrying Assault Boat (Navy)
LCOL	Lieutenant Colonel
LNO	Liaison Officer
LPL-30	Laser Pointer
LRRP	Long Range Recon Patrol
LRSLC	Long Range Surveillance Leader Course
LTC	Lieutenant Colonel
LZ	Landing Zone
M-1950	Weapons carrying case (airborne)

M-2	.50 cal Machine Gun
M-203	Grenade launcher
M240G	7.62 machine gun
M-60	7.62 machine gun
MAJ	Major
MFFJM	Military Freefall Jumpmaster
MG	Major General
MIA	Missing In Action
MK-19	Grenade launcher
MOUT	Military Operations in Urban Terrain
MP	Military Police
M-577	Armored Command Post vehicle
MTT	Mobile Training Team
NCO	Non-Commissioned Officer
NCOIC	Non-Commissioned Officer In Charge
NTC	National Training Center
NVG	Night vision goggles
OCS	Officer Candidate School
OIC	Officer in Charge
OPFOR	Opposing Forces
OPORD	Operations Order
PFC	Private First Class
PL	Platoon Leader
POMCUS	Pre-positioning of Material Configured in Unit Sets
POW	Prisoner Of War
PT	Physical Training
PVS-7	Night Vision Goggles
PZ	Pick-up Zone
RE	Recovery Element
REFORGER	Return of Forces to Germany
RI	Ranger Instructor
RIP	Ranger Indoctrination Program

ROTC	Reserve Officer Training Corp
RRF1	Ranger Readiness Force One
RSOV	Ranger Special Operations Vehicle
RTO	Radio and Telephone Operator
S-3	Operations Officer
SAS	Special Air Services
SAW	Squad Automatic Weapon
SDO	Staff Duty Officer
SF	Special Forces
SFC	Sergeant First Class (E7)
SGT	Sergeant (E5)
SITREP	Situation Report
SOP	Standard Operating Procedures
SPIE	Small Patrol Infiltration or Exfiltration Rig
SSG	Staff Sergeant (E6)
SWC	Special Warfare Center
T-55	Russian Tank
TOC	Tactical Operations Center
TVD	Tennessee Valley Divide
U(M)H-60	Black hawk helicopter
UXO	Unexploded Ordnance

About the Author

Major David A. Combs entered the United States Army on 22 August 1985. He attended Basic Training and Advanced Individual Training at Fort Sill, Oklahoma. He graduated from the Officer Candidate School and was commissioned a Second Lieutenant in 1991.

Major Combs assignments included: Fire Support Sergeant, A-Company, 3/75 Ranger Battalion; Senior Fire Support Sergeant, 75th Ranger Regiment, Fort Benning, GA; Colt Team Leader and Battalion Fire Support Officer, 3/29 Field Artillery, 4th ID, Fort Carson, CO; Fire Support Officer, C-Company, 2/75 Ranger Battalion, Fort Lewis, WA; Battery Commander, 1-15th Field Artillery, 2nd Infantry Division, Camp Casey, Korea; Army ROTC Instructor, University of Northern Iowa, Cedar Falls, IA; POW/MIA Team Leader, Joint Task Force Full

Accounting, Camp H.M. Smith, HI; Assistant S-3, 25th ID(L) DivArty, Schofield Barracks, HI; Strategic Planner, Combined Forces Command - Afghanistan.

His military and civilian education achievements include: Bachelor of Science Degree, Officer Candidate School, Field Artillery Officer Basic Course, Field Artillery Officer Advance Course, Command and General Staff College. Military Schools include: Ranger, Pathfinder, Air Assault, Airborne, and Military Free Fall.

Awards include: the Bronze Star Medal, Defense Meritorious Service Medal, Meritorious Service Medal (2), Army Commendation Medal (6), Joint Service Achievement Medal (3), Army Achievement Medal (6), Armed Forces Expeditionary Medal (2) with Arrowhead Device and Bronze Service Star, Humanitarian Service Medal, Global War On Terrorism Service Medal, Global War On Terrorism Expeditionary Medal, Afghanistan Campaign Medal, and Bronze Service Star (Combat Parachute Jump).

He now continues to serve the United States military as a contractor in both Afghanistan and Iraq.